Beginning the Journey

From Infant Baptism
to First Eucharist

Department of Education
United States Catholic Conference

In the 1992 plans and programs of the Department of Education, as approved by the Committee on Education, provision was made for printed materials dealing with the spiritual development of young children from birth to first eucharist. *Beginning the Journey: From Infant Baptism to First Eucharist* is intended to offer guidance to parents, catechists, and teachers. This document has been reviewed and approved by the Most Reverend Robert J. Banks, chairman of the Committee on Education, and is authorized for publication by the undersigned.

Monsignor Robert N. Lynch
General Secretary
September 27, 1994   NCCB/USCC

BV
1475.2
.B43
1994

ISBN 1-55586-527-5

Contents

Foreword

Beginning the Journey: From Infant Baptism to First Eucharist is intended to be of assistance to parents, catechists, and teachers as they guide the development of the spiritual life of children from its beginning until the time of first eucharist. We know this is a sensitive and fruitful time for formation and that children have a special capacity for the things of the spirit.

There is no intention here to romanticize or glamorize childhood. For many children, it is a difficult period and a time of suffering. War, violence, poor nutrition, poverty, family breakdown, domestic abuse, and lack of health and educational opportunities have a more profound impact on children than on any other segment of society. Some children develop within a happier set of circumstances, sustained by a stable home and necessary resources. For all children, however, their need for the spiritual is as great as that of adults.

The recent publication of the U.S. Catholic bishops *Follow the Way of Love: A Pastoral Message to Families* urges children and youth to accompany their parents and elders in the way of holiness (cf. p. 27). It is hoped that the words that follow will offer opportunity for reflection, guidance, and support to those who point out the way of holiness to children.

"Let the children come to me; do not stop them; for it is to such as these that the kingdom of God belongs" (Mk 10:14).

Infant Baptism and the Process of Christian Initiation

by Robert D. Duggan

> The lived experience of the family and the child before, during, and after the ritual celebration will speak most eloquently about the nature of faith, what it means to be church, how God's saving love is revealed, wherein lies a Christian's commitment to mission. . . .

When Pope John XXIII announced the convocation of a great ecumenical council in 1959, he used the image of opening up windows to allow fresh breezes of renewal to blow through the Church. Neither the saintly pope nor anyone else suspected at that point how quickly and how far the forces of reform and renewal would spread.

Renewal and Revitalization

Among the chief instruments of renewal was a mandate by the Fathers of the Council to reform the entire liturgical life of the Church. And, among the many aspects of that liturgical reform, none was more important than the decision to revitalize the sacraments of Christian initiation. The restoration of the integrity and sequence of the sacraments of initiation (baptism-confirmation-eucharist) was accomplished most dramatically in the creation of an entirely new ritual for use with adults. Popularly called the RCIA (*Rite of Christian Initiation of Adults*), that ritual has awakened and shaped an awareness of how one comes to the fullness of Christian faith in a way few dreamed possible. In parishes across the United States and around the world, communities have come to experience and understand, in an entirely new

Robert D. Duggan, a sacramental theologian, is pastor of St. Rose of Lima Church in Gaithersburg, Maryland.

way, the process of initiation and the rituals that incorporate a person into full membership in the Church.

The RCIA, as the Church's premier initiatory statement, continues to yield new insights and revitalize the many other ways that we bring people into our Church. The practice of infant baptism, confirmation of the young, and celebration of first eucharist are all undergoing scrutiny and renewal in light of the results experienced by those implementing the RCIA. Theologians speak of the "normative status" of adult initiation, but it is the practical success of the RCIA on the local level that is truly responsible for the widespread influences that it exerts in increasing measure.

*Appropriate catechesis will help parents
to explore their deepest longings for their
child, to sort out the many "wants"
created by a consumerist culture, and to
respond at the level of ultimate concern.*

Individuals and communities have discovered the deep meaning of initiation; they have been touched by the power of its rituals: they have seen how it brings to faith not only those coming into membership, but also the community into which they are initiated. In light of such powerful experiences of transformation, many are asking how this same dynamism can be shared with our young as they, too, are brought to full membership in a similar process of initiation.

This collection of essays, in its own way, reflects one aspect of an awareness that has been sharpened in us all as a result of the RCIA. More than ever before, we are reminded that initiation—for our young as well as for adults—is a *gradual process* that must be supported and nurtured by prayer and pastoral care over a long period of time. The inspiration for this book and the evolution of pastoral sensitivity and insight manifest in its individual chapters give eloquent testimony to how well we are learning the lessons of initiation taught to us in the RCIA. Each author has a particular perspective, but all of them are convinced that the process of initiation for our young goes forward, for better or for worse, in crucial fashion during the time between the sacraments of baptism and first eucharist. In one sense, the material in this volume might be considered a series of initiatory strategies for those who work with our young and their families between those ritual moments.

Rite of Infant Baptism

In the present chapter, the author wishes to focus on the rite of infant baptism from the perspective of a sacramental theologian. That perspective will be presented in a way that is consistent with the theological vision of the RCIA. Any attempt to interpret a text (in this case, the "text" is the ritual of infant baptism) apart from its broader context is doomed to a narrow, myopic reading. It is hoped that the understanding of the celebration of baptism for infants that is developed in these pages will be enriched by the full scope of the liturgical renewal of Vatican II, of which the reform of the sacraments of initiation is such a vital part, and of which the RCIA is one of the finest fruits. The broader context out of which we operate here, then, represents the collective wisdom of an ecclesial and liturgical renewal process of nearly three decades' duration.

We have already indicated above how we have come to understand that initiation is a gradual process, not a discrete event coterminous with any particular ritual. This is a foundational insight with broad implications. We realize better than ever before, for example, that any liturgical celebration marks only one moment in a reality that is much larger. And, in order to understand adequately (from either a pastoral or theological perspective) what a given rite is about, one must carefully consider all that leads up to it as well as all that flows from it. In our reflection on infant baptism, this means that we must look at the pastoral process that leads a family to request baptism for their child, as well as how both the community and the family take steps—after the baptism—to develop and live out the meanings celebrated in the rite. Only within such a broad framework do the symbols, texts, and ritual gestures of the celebration make sense.

Once upon a time, people were satisfied with the notion that "baptism takes away original sin" as justification for celebrating the sacrament with our infants. It mattered little how well prepared families were to undertake the responsibilities of Christian parenting, nor how likely anyone was to follow through on the implications of the child's incorporation into the Body of Christ.

What mattered was removing the "stain," and the pouring of water accompanied by the proper words accomplished that perfectly. All else was secondary, to the point of being neglected pretty much entirely. The water rite was the "moment" that counted, and there was scarcely a thought given to an initiatory process.

The RCIA has taught us otherwise. The ritual of infant baptism is part of an initiatory process that extends from the first moment parents are aware of the pregnancy through the early years of a child's life. Both the community and the child's family must prepare themselves in order to celebrate properly a ritual that holds such promise. Pastoral care, evangelizing proclamation, and careful catechesis are all necessary activities of a community that wishes to engage properly in the sacramental ritual. And afterwards, ideally, both the community and the family are expected to continue a process of reflection and growth rooted in what they have experienced in the celebration. Mystagogical catechesis in this instance includes a range of activities that affect the growing child and its family over a span of years. Thus conceived, the celebration of infant baptism is a nodal event in the life of a particular family and a parish that spawns a whole way of being, not only for the child and its family but also for the community at large. Just as the family at baptism accepts responsibility for being the domestic church in which the child's faith will receive primary formation, so too does the larger community accept its role in an initiatory process that will be ongoing for years.

An Intimate Connection

One of the important learnings that has come from the implementation of the RCIA in recent years is the intimate connection that must exist between the catechesis which leads up to a particular celebration and the specific symbols and gestures which make up that ritual. In a certain sense, everything that is done prior to the celebration of the sacrament is meant to enable the participants to enter fully and meaningfully into the words and actions of the rite. "Ritual catechesis" is a new term often used to express the intricate interaction required between catechesis and ritual in this context. An older approach that emphasized "sacramental preparation" concentrated its energies on instructing and informing the participants about the theology of the sacrament in question and devoted very little attention to what was actually to occur in the ritual itself. Many a sacramental preparation program today still places little emphasis on the major symbols and ritual gestures that will constitute the participants' actual experience of the sacramental rite.

> *In the case of infant baptism, it is the faith of both the parents and the community that is at issue.*

Ritual catechesis, on the other hand, takes as its starting point the lived experience of the sacrament and tries to minister pastorally and catechetically in ways that will prepare the participants to maximize their authentic engagement in the rite and its attendant meanings. This means, for example, that instead of a series of instructions on the ancient tradition of tracing a cross on one preparing for baptism, catechesis is offered which prepares parents to accept the meaning of such a gesture and which sensitizes them to the ways our rituals use nonverbals, such as touch, to communicate deep meanings. Afterwards, following the experience, further catechesis and pastoral care help to unpack those deeper meanings embedded in our ritual tradition.

Given this approach, what shape might the pastoral care take which is offered to parents seeking baptism for their infant? The answer to such a question lies in an analysis of the rite itself and the multiple meanings encoded in its ritual form. The question to be asked by those designing a parish-based preparation experience should be: How can we help all of the participants to enter most deeply into the meaning of this rite? The ritual begins with a question to the parents regarding what it is they seek for their child. Appropriate catechesis will help parents to explore their deepest longings for their child, to sort out the many "wants" created by a consumerist culture, and to respond at the level of ultimate concern. As a first gesture of acceptance, the presider and then the parents trace a cross on the child. What a marvelously shocking gesture. If they are to experience the wrenching ambiguity with which Christian tradition surrounds the cross as symbol of both death and victory, parents will need to be led carefully to the decision that only by way of the cross does this child's destiny include the glory of resurrection. Parents represent the most fiercely instinctive urge of our species to protect the newborn. What level of faith and what level of awareness is required for new parents to trace on their helpless infant a symbol of capital punishment? What sort of pastoral dialogue and what form of proclamation of the Christian mystery must be offered by a parish community in order to help the parents experience the full power of that ritual gesture?

In similar fashion, we might ask what sort of preparation must be offered to the godparents, to extended family members, and to the community at large if their involvement in the ritual is to be fully participative and meaningful. The strategies required in these instances would obviously extend well beyond the limits of a few "sessions" for prospective parents. In order to awaken a parish community to its real responsibility for the ongoing nurture of new parents and the early faith formation of their children, long-range efforts need to be put in place at several levels of parish life. In how many parishes do people still avoid the baptism Mass because it adds an extra ten or fifteen minutes to their Sunday worship? Such attitudes are symptomatic of a catastrophic condition within a faith community, yet we tolerate them as "normal." Rather, they should incite us to the urgency of the task that must be accomplished if we are ever to celebrate the initiation of infants in credible fashion. Careful thought, creative efforts, patience, and persistence are all needed to raise the consciousness of a community at large regarding the essential role they play both in the liturgy of baptism and in the pastoral care that must follow in subsequent years. Lacking such awareness and commitment on the part of the larger community, the celebration of infant baptism will inevitably have something of a hollow ring to it, much as would Sunday eucharist in a segregated community where everyone knows that no one intends to change their racist behaviors.

The Importance of Lived Experience

Those with extensive experience of the RCIA have gradually come to see that its rituals enact an operative theology (of Church, ministry, God, salvation, and so forth) that is often at some variance with the neat synthesis found in textbooks or catechisms. They have also discovered that it is always people's lived experience that will win out over abstract notions contained in a prepared lesson. The same insight is equally valid with the first sacramental ritual marking the beginning of a child's initiation process. The lived experience of the family and the child before, during, and after the ritual celebration will speak most eloquently about the nature of faith, what it means to be church, how God's saving love is revealed, wherein lies a Christian's commitment to mission, and so forth. A parish can supply new parents with bright pamphlets describing a "new" theology of baptism as sacrament of belonging to the Christian community; but, if baptism is still celebrated apart from the regular assembly of the community— often in a dark corner of an empty church—then the empty character of those bright promises will be all the more starkly evident. If the lived experience of new parents is one of total neglect following the baptismal ceremony, then no words about the community's commitment of support will convince them. If we say that baptism is the foundational sacrament of Christian life, but we celebrate it liturgically without any of the care we might normally extend to an important occasion, then our words become simply incredible.

A renewed theology of infant baptism requires that we be much more attentive to what we do and how we do it. Unless and until our liturgical experience of the sacrament employs full and robust symbols, in a celebration where the participants act as if they fully believed this is a moment of ultimate grace, our verbiage will remain just another form of sacramental nominalism. Baptism, even infant baptism, is a sacrament of faith that requires the active presence of a believing community. If our operative theology as enacted in celebration after celebration signals the opposite, why are we surprised when nothing seems to happen as the result of our ministrations? A richly expressive celebration by an assembly of true believers is the norm toward which all of our pastoral and catechetical efforts must aim. Similarly, unless there is a substantive experience of a parish's commitment to initiate a child into a faith community during the years between baptism and first eucharist, our protestations of concern will fall on deaf ears. If a renewed theology of infant baptism as a sacrament which begins a process of initiation is ever to sound credible, our communities must be prepared to put forth the kind of efforts described elsewhere in this volume.

A Covenant Community

The notion of covenant is one of the strongest biblical motifs found in our baptismal heritage. Scriptural readings assigned for baptism frequently include covenant stories; ancient baptismal iconography abounded in symbols of covenant; prayer texts fairly echo with references to baptism as God's covenant with us; and reams of theological explanations are available in which the dynamics of covenant relationships are applied to the effects of the sacrament. In the Judeo-Christian tradition, entrance into covenantal relationship with God has always been accomplished by becoming part of a faith community. This critical notion continues to hold the key to a renewal in our theology and praxis of infant baptism. Without faith, sacraments become magical gestures; without community, they are reduced to a privatistic and individualistic form of religious behavior that is contrary to our entire tradition. In the case of infant baptism, it is the faith of both the parents and the community that is at issue. Likewise, the covenant community that provides the setting for that faith is both the family (as domestic church) and the larger community represented by the liturgical assembly.

*Imagine how powerful an experience
it would be for a child if its parents
continued to trace a cross on the forehead
as they did during the baptismal liturgy,
every evening at bedtime. . . .*

The network of relationships that are both formed and expressed in the liturgical ritual must be attended to very carefully. There is the parent/child relationship; the godparent/godchild relationship; the relationship of the parents with the local community of faith and vice versa; there is the larger community of the Church—embracing the entire communion of saints as it relates to the participants in a particular celebration; there is the presider who acts *in persona Christi* as pastoral leader for the child, the child's family, and the community at large; and, of course, there is the graced relationship with God which is effected by the gift of the Spirit and is shared by the entire assembly of believers. Faith is the matrix that makes of all these relationships an experience of God's salvation. Covenant is the notion that reminds us how it is that faith results in such relationships as these where commitment and fidelity are required.

These ideas are particularly apropos to the topic of this book, which aims to explore how a community carries forward the initiatory process in the years between the ritual of baptism and first eucharist. The covenant relationship forged in faith at the ritual of baptism is not just between the child and God. Just as surely, there are bonds formed between the child, the child's parents, and the community that welcomes the child. As in every covenant relationship, there are mutual responsibilities undertaken and commitments made which will define and shape the relationship across the coming years. An attentive reading of the ritual text makes clear the collaborative nature of the project of Christian formation undertaken by parents and the larger community on behalf of the child. The scope of that mutual commitment is explored in the other chapters of this book.

In celebrating the rites of the RCIA process, it is clear beyond mistake that following the ritual (e.g., after the Rite of Acceptance, Election, & Scrutiny, etc.) the community will continue its ministry through a variety of initiatory processes. The pastoral directives within the RCIA even spell out in some detail many of the forms these initiatory efforts should take. In the same way, following the celebration of infant baptism, both the domestic church (the family) and the larger community bear a responsibility to collaborate in nurturing the faith of the child through appropriate initiatory strategies. From the viewpoint of the parish community, this means that efforts must be directed both toward assisting the parents and toward the child's growing faith experience. It is truly remarkable how little awareness of this responsibility is apparent in most parish communities.

Symbols and Faith Formation

The problem, of course, is that our understanding of faith formation has been so closely wedded to an academic model of religious education. In most parishes there is virtually nothing available for children or their parents in the years between baptism and first eucharist. This is all the more incredible when one realizes that those early years of childhood are precisely the time when a child's basic religious categories are being formed. The religious imagination is being filled with vivid and indelible notions of God, church, sacrament, and so forth, yet in parish after parish there is a complete absence of any intentional effort to initiate children carefully and thoughtfully during these early years.

Wisdom gleaned from experience with the RCIA would say that initiatory formation during this period needs to build on the meanings celebrated symbolically in the child's baptismal ceremony. Mystagogical catechesis, as the RCIA would term these efforts, would be the primary focus of the community's efforts during the "in-between" years. (The term "mystagogical catechesis" refers in the strict sense to what occurs during the fifty days of Easter, immediately following full initiation at the Easter Vigil. Its use here, however, is by extension and is meant to highlight a certain continuity of approach in initiatory strategies for both children and adults.) In essence, this refers to a form of catechesis that takes as its point of departure the actual celebration of the sacrament itself and concentrates its energies on helping the newly baptized to understand the full meaning of the symbols and rituals, the prayers and readings, which were used in the baptismal liturgy.

In fact, since the liturgy of baptism contains our most basic sacramental symbols and proclaims the fundamental Christian story, it is a natural source for the sort of mystagogical catechesis that we envision. Water, oil, light, touch, (if celebrated at eucharist, add bread and wine), white garment, word proclaimed, faith professed, community gathering and processing, promises made and evil rejected, all of these and more provide the "stuff" for a rich mystagogical catechesis of the young child and its parents in those early formative years.

The imaginative world of children revels in the ambiguity of our primordial symbols. The prayer of blessing over the baptismal water is filled with allusions to water as source of life, destroying flood, gateway to the promised land, sacrificial offering, and so forth. As children experience the miracle of rain that produces growth, as they are introduced to the awesome power of the sea, as they are bathed and refreshed, as they experience terror from slipping beneath the waters of their first swimming pool, as they sail paper boats and splash and play, countless connections can be made with the rich heritage of water symbols so prevalent in our baptismal liturgy.

Imagine how powerful an experience it would be for a child if its parents continued to trace a cross on the forehead as they did during the baptismal liturgy, every evening at bedtime, or during times of shared prayer or to accompany words of blessing during times of illness or injury. As the child grows and begins to question the meaning and background of that gentle parental touch, imagine the explanations and connections that could be offered. Imagine, too, the powerful moment of recognition that symbol would hold for the child when the baptism of a younger sibling occurs, or when the priest's blessing at the end of Sunday Mass is identified as a similar gesture, or when the bishop's touch with chrism at confirmation evokes a flood of memories. Mystagogical catechesis as part of the initiatory process involves a "layering" of meanings by virtue of repetitive experience and accompanying explanations that gradually expand the horizons of Christian meaning for a child. Parishes might regularly hold sessions for parents to introduce them to storytelling skills and to help them learn how to weave the tales of our Judeo-Christian Scriptures into the fabric of their children's imaginative world. In such situations, parents, as much as children, would be the recipients of mystagogical catechesis. We are reminded that our earliest examples of mystagogia were homilies preached purportedly to the neophytes, but in actuality were directed equally to the rest of the faithful. Just so, a parish's efforts to unpack for its children the meaning of their baptismal liturgy will actually profit parents as much as their children.

Conclusion

In order to accomplish the vision being offered in these pages, religious education professionals, liturgists, and pastoral care generalists will need to collaborate in developing teachable moments, programs, celebrations, and myriad other initiatory strategies. Our parishes will need to devote as much time and energy to spiritual formation during these earliest childhood years as they have in the past to the parochial school or the CCD scope and sequence chart. In doing so, a baptismal praxis will evolve that will give new meaning to our understanding of Christian initiation. We will be theologizing not out of textbook answers but out of a lived experience that is richly varied and deep with commitment. Our traditional notions of faith, covenant, community, even salvation, will take on a power and an immediacy that might at present seem impossible. When an entire community accepts its responsibility to initiate its young from baptism onwards, there will be significant, even dramatic changes effected in parish life. Communities across our nation and around the world have already experienced the revitalizing effect of a commitment to initiate adults in the RCIA process. We can only dream of the impact on our parishes when we make a commitment to initiate our young according to a similar vision.

Suggested Reading

Coles, Robert. *The Spiritual Life of Children.* Boston, Mass.: Houghton-Mifflin, 1990.

Duffy, Regis, ed. *Alternative Futures for Worship,* Vol. 1, "General Introduction." Collegeville, Minn.: The Liturgical Press, 1987.

Duggan, Robert and Maureen Kelly. *The Christian Initiation of Children: For the Future.* Ramsey, N.J.: Paulist Press, 1991.

Guzie, Tad. *The Book of Sacramental Basics.* Ramsey, N.J.: Paulist Press, 1981.

Searle, Mark, ed. *Alternative Futures for Worship,* Vol. 2, "Baptism and Confirmation." Collegeville, Minn.: The Liturgical Press, 1987.

_____. *Christening: The Making of Christians.* Collegeville, Minn.: Liturgical Press, 1980.

The Original and Irreplaceable Catechist: The Parent!

by Lorraine P. Amendolara

Effective parenting skills, contrary to popular myths, are not inborn. Maternal or paternal instincts don't necessarily "kick in" with know-how and wisdom when needed.

It "Runs" in the Family

A little girl who was in a class to prepare her for the reception of the sacrament of the eucharist was asked by her teacher if she believed in God. The child quickly responded, "Yes, I do!"

"Well," said the teacher, "why do you believe in God?"

The answer was a little slower this time, "I don't know why," the child finally said. "I think it runs in our family."

It's amazing what "runs" in families. A young boy walks with the exact same gait as his dad; a teenager's voice is mistaken for that of her mother's by a caller; an entire family might have the very same mannerisms. Besides acquiring some superficial characteristics of her family, this little girl—between the sacraments of baptism and eucharist—has learned the values, attitudes, and beliefs about life, death, sex, herself, others, and God that "run" in her family.

Rhetoric vs. Reality

Our Church has written, quite eloquently and powerfully, about the family in many of its documents. One of its most provocative statements comes from *Lumen Gentium*, which refers to the family as

Lorraine P. Amendolara is a noted author and an associate superintendent of schools for the Diocese of Metuchen.

the domestic church (cf. no. 11). The statement is not worded in the form of a simile. The family is not "like," or just "part of" the Church, but is, in fact, the domestic church.

Yet, we cannot speak about the importance of the family without recognizing the role of the parent as the "architect of family life." Indeed, the parents are pastors of the domestic church. They are, according to *Lumen Gentium*, " . . . by word and example, the first heralds of the faith with regard to their children" (no. 11).

This stress on the significance of the parents as the primary and dominant religious educator is noted in other documents:

> . . . [T]hey [parents] should realize that they are thereby cooperating with the love of God the Creator and are, in a certain sense, its interpreters (*Pastoral on the Church in the Modern World*, no. 50).

> Parents are first and foremost catechists of their children. They catechize informally, but powerfully by example and instruction (*National Catechetical Directory*, no. 212).

> Education in the faith by parents . . . a witness that is often without words but which perseveres throughout a day-to-day life lived in accordance with the gospel (*On Catechesis in Our Time*, no. 68).

> The ministry of evangelization carried out by Christian parents is original and irreplaceable. It assumes the characteristics of the family itself, which should be interwoven with love, simplicity, practicality and daily witness (*Familiaris Consortio*, no. 53).

What our Church in all her wisdom is saying, over and over, is that there is a great drama being played out in the midst of daily life. The parents are, in a sense, the playwrights of that drama. They are creating the script for their children. Parents are interpreting God's love for their children. They are catechizing their children informally, but powerfully, often providing a witness that is without words. As Robert Fulgum advises parents: "Don't worry that your children never listen to you. Worry that they are always watching you." The parent, because of his or her intimate and matchless relationship with the child, is indeed the "original and irreplaceable catechist." How does reality measure up to this dynamic and forceful rhetoric?

In 1978, the National Conference of Catholic Bishops' *Plan of Pastoral Action for Family Ministry* targeted six areas of national need, one of which was a ministry to parents. The Parent Education Ministry of the Archdiocese of New York was created in 1979 as a direct response to that plan. Although it has been over a dozen years since the bishops promulgated that plan, a ministry to parents in this country remains underdeveloped. While several dioceses are initiating ministries to parents, on the whole, they are underserviced and, in many instances, totally neglected. This reality stands in sharp contrast to the rhetoric.

The question often arises, "Why should there be a ministry to parents? Shouldn't parents know instinctively how to bring up children?" It seems that if you are a human being, you should have the qualifications to raise another one! Unfortunately, children are not born or adopted with manuals, guidebooks, or instructions. Effective parenting skills, contrary to popular myths, are not inborn. Maternal or paternal instinct does not necessarily "kick in" with know-how and wisdom when needed.

Consider the gamut of parenting possibilities—single parenting, building families through adoption, step-parenting, parenting learning disabled or handicapped children, grandparenting, and so forth. Who or what prepares one or sustains one for these situations? Chilling statistics regarding fragmented family relationships—child neglect and abuse, teenage runaways, throwaways and suicide, to name a few—all attest to the crisis that exists in families today.

Father Thomas Lynch writes of this crisis:

> Although there may be an expectation of intimacy, members will have little ability or energy to achieve it. Their homes become motels; their cars, taxis, their tables, fast food restaurants.... The family, then, is chaotic, and non-relational in its mode of operation.[1]

Our Church devotes so much of its resources to education and rightly so. However, let's draw a few comparisons.

Think of the investment the Church makes in those who have a vocation to the priesthood. Years (six to eight and more) of preparation, education, and nurturing are provided in order to receive the sacrament of holy orders. Yet, those of us called to marriage and parenting also receive a sacrament. That sacrament involves not only giving life, but cherishing and training that life over the developmental cycles. Although marriage preparation programs have improved, many parents recall their sacramental preparation as a one-day Pre-Cana conference where they heard they should have children, but not necessarily what they should do with the children after they arrived. Reflect on what the Church teaches about the importance of the parents' role and then compare this with the tremendous imbalance in the sacramental preparation for other lifetime vocations.

Another comparison: in educational circles, it is customary for teachers to cultivate expertise not only in particular content areas but also with certain age levels. A highly skilled junior high school teacher might vehemently object to a proposed change by the principal to teach a kindergarten class saying, "I don't know anything about early childhood education!" Suppose a diocese was mandating a sex education curriculum in all schools. Imagine a principal asking a social studies teacher to become the coordinator of sex education for the school. The teacher might protest: "I don't know anything about how to communicate sex ed to kids. I refuse to do it!" Or at the very least, the teacher might say: "I'll consider doing it only if you send me for training."

Yet, parents are expected to be skilled in dealing with all stages of child development: infancy, toddlerhood, school-age children, and then shift gears for adolescence. Further, they are expected to teach their children about religion, death, sex, and so forth, without anyone enabling or empowering them to tackle such important and intimate topics.

Many dioceses, concerned about the quality of religious education programs, mandate or strongly suggest that catechists in schools and religious education programs go through training and certification programs. This is wonderful. But if we really believe that the parent catechizes informally but powerfully and is the original and irreplaceable catechist, what are we doing to help them?

Parenting must be seen as the important and sacred vocation it is. Its status in the Church and society should be elevated.

Sometimes it seems as if the main event in religious education of children takes place in the Catholic school or the catechetical program since that is where all the energies and resources are focused. Family life is just a side show to the main event. Yet, the *National Catechetical Directory* points out:

Though the influence of peers and of adult catechists is important, catechetical programs are not intended to supplant parents as the primary educators of their children (no. 229).

Despite this position, catechetical programs have superseded and displaced parents and relegated them to the sidelines where many are content to be.

Parent Education: An "Up the River" Ministry

Since parent education is a relatively new and underdeveloped ministry in the Church, its critical importance to our Church and society can be best illustrated through the following story:

One beautiful summer day, a man went to the banks of a nearby river to relax, have some lunch, and commune with God in nature. He found the perfect spot, spread a red checkered table cloth, and opened his wicker picnic basket, which held fruit, wine, cheese, and bread. He settled down savoring the food and the scenery.

Suddenly, the peace and quiet of this idyllic setting were shattered. He heard screams. There was a man in the river. He was flailing his arms and screaming: "Help me! I'm drowning! I can't swim! Help me!"

Our friend jumped up and ran into the river, his heart pounding furiously. He was able to grab the man and pull him ashore. However, he wasn't breathing; he seemed lifeless. Our friend proceeded to give him mouth-to-mouth resuscitation.

Just as this man revived and our friend was feeling a tremendous sense of relief and accomplishment, he heard screaming again. He looked up to see another man in the river. His arms flailing, he was shouting: "Help me! I'm drowning! I can't swim! Help me!"

Our friend geared up again. All his psychic and physical energies were focused on saving this man. Yet, this time it was more difficult. The man was further out in the river. The currents were stronger. However, our friend did reach him and brought him back to shore. This second man, like the first, needed mouth-to-mouth resuscitation. Finally, the man revived and our friend felt both relieved and dissipated. His energy was sapped.

Just as he began to help these men to their feet, screams were heard again. "Help me! I'm drowning! I can't swim! Help me!" Another man was in the river. Our friend didn't know whether he would have the strength to save this third man. He wondered whether he would drown himself if he attempted to rescue him. Yet, he went into the river again. Suddenly, in a flash, there was a revelation. "Dear Lord," he said, "I'm so busy saving these men that I'm not looking up the river to see who or what is pushing them in!"

As a Church and society, we can never cease our efforts at crisis intervention. However, we will never win the battle against the militating forces that assault our young people today—fragmented family relationships, chemical dependency, abuse of all kinds, teenage pregnancy, and suicide—if we don't take a long, hard look "up the river" and see the family. Since parents are the architects of family life, we must begin while the child is still in the womb or when a couple is waiting for an adoption. If we want to reach the children, we must first reach their parents.

The Church as Mother needs to nurture these nurturers of Catholic family life. The Church as Teacher needs to educate and support parents as they journey with their children to the Lord through the heartwarming and heartwrenching experiences of parenting. Parent education, then, is an "up the river" ministry aimed at keeping families healthy and well functioning and ultimately preventing family members from falling in the river.

Parents must hear, repeatedly and unmistakably, from the Church that they have a sacred and heroic vocation. Perhaps then, they will come to believe it. Unfortunately, there are still remnants of the influence of monasticism that have negatively influenced the development of a spirituality of all baptized persons. To follow the Lord in the monastic life, one had to flee the world, renounce one's family, find solitude, and live ascetically. Since this kind of existence is impossible for the parents of infants and toddlers—for all parents, for that matter—they fail to believe that they are called to holiness in another way; they fail to see the spiritual dimension of their lives.

Parents' call to holiness involves, not renouncing their families, but embracing their families as the locus of God's presence. Not escaping the noise and the din of the world to find God in solitude, but finding God in the midst of the noise and din; in the midst of the cuddling and hugging; in the midst of the temper tantrums and sleepless nights; in the midst of unpaid bills and bursting pipes. This is a tremendous challenge—to probe beneath the surface of daily life and discover the Lord in our midst.

Many fail to see the significance of the vocation of parenting. Yet when Jesus was asked by his disciples, "Who is the greatest in the kingdom of heaven?" (Mt 18:1-2), he gave them a very radical answer—not a king or a rabbi, but a child! Who gives life to, cherishes, nurtures, and trains the child, the greatest in the kingdom—parents! Parenting must be seen as the important and sacred vocation it is. Its status in the Church and society should be elevated.

The Original and Irreplaceable Catechist

The U.S. Catholic bishops in the document *The Challenge of Peace* said to parents: "Children hear the Gospel first from your lips" (no. 306). Indeed, the root meaning of the word *catechesis* is "to echo." As life and its meaning unfold for children, parents act as "theologians in residence."

However, since parents have been treated by Catholic schools and catechetical programs as simply adjuncts to the faith development of the children, they neither feel prepared nor competent in sharing their faith with their children.

It is the parent who acts as an evangelist, inviting the child into a loving relationship into the Lord.

Religious education has been formalized to such a degree that parents feel uncomfortable and hesitant in their role as catechetist because they haven't studied theology or perhaps are unsure of their beliefs so they say to the professionals: "You do it!"

However, faith development begins with the first feeding and first holding, not the first religious lesson. James Fowler in *Stages of Faith* claims that,

We all begin the pilgrimage of faith as infants. . . . If there is not enough holding, rocking, or stimulation from communication, our adaptive capacities for relationship and loving attachments can be severely retarded or non-activated. . . . [2]

So faith development begins in simplicity, with rocking, holding, feeding, listening, cuddling, forgiving, comforting. These things that parents do every day become springboards of faith. Nothing needs to be superimposed on family life to teach children about a bountiful, loving, compassionate God—no theological treatises or discourses. In doing the "little things" well, the mundane of everyday life can become miraculous!

Those professionals who are charged with religious education would do well to reflect on the following passage, whose author is anonymous:

> And Jesus said,
> "Who do you say I am?"
> And they answered,
> "You are the eschatological
> manifestation of the ground
> of our being, the *kerygma*
> in which we found the
> ultimate meaning of our
> interpersonal relationship."
> And Jesus said,
> *"What?"*

The most powerful messages children learn are oftentimes through wordless messages. Father Andrew Greeley points out that children

> . . . watch in fascination the story their parents are telling. The underlying theme of hope or despair, of graciousness or absurdity which runs through the parental story is surely communicated. . . . The religious imagination of young people is powerfully influenced by what goes on in the family of origin.[3]

It is in the everyday, common experiences that parents and children discover and develop their faith in God. Lucie Barber in *The Religious Education of Pre-School Children* discusses six reasons why the parents' role in religious education is so critical:

1. Parents want what is best for their children—including the best religious education possible.

2. Parents are ripe for learning. Parenthood, as well as childhood, is chock full of "teachable moments" for both parents and children. Those "teachable moments" should be seized.

3. Parents are natural teachers of their children and they begin teaching from the moment of birth or adoption onward. The sheer delight parents express in their children's accomplishments provides the fuel necessary to keep them growing well.

4. Parents have "intimacy power." They have more physical contact with their child than anyone else.

5. Parents know their children best and are ego-involved. This special relationship provides the arena for marvelous learning experiences.

6. Parents recognize their child's uniqueness. They provide "individualized instruction" as no other teacher can.[4]

Clearly, the parental role in the child's early religious education is pivotal to faith development. It is the parent who acts as an evangelist, inviting the child into a loving relationship with the Lord.

A Shift in Focus

The Chinese word for *crisis* is composed of two symbols. One stands for *danger*, the other for *opportunity*. There are those who claim that family life in our country is in a state of crisis. Those that suffer the most from this crisis are the children. The well-being of their minds, bodies, and spirits is in danger.

However, opportunities exist to change the course of the present crisis. While children are always at the heart of our educational energies as a church, we must shift the focus from solely educating children to educating the adults who are responsible for those children—parents as well as teachers.

When you educate a parent, you educate generations of children to come. In *Familiaris Consortio*, Pope John Paul II wrote, "The future function of the world and of the Church passes through the family" (no. 75).

The primary change agents in any society are not the presidents, cardinals, or CEOs. The primary change agents are parents and teachers. They fashion the future through their children. Their impact is felt through what they have taught their children about love, hate, peace, sexism, racism, materialism, the environment, and so forth.

Church ministers—priests, catechists, educators, youth ministers—must think "big." They need to think systemically. The family must be viewed as a dynamic, pulsating, growing system; and we need to minister to that family "up the river."

The task of church ministers is not to do the job of religious education for the parents, but to do it with them and, most of all, to enable them to do the job themselves.

Church ministers, from the pulpit, in the media, in the classrooms, and in conversations, need to elevate the status of parenting. The reality must begin to match the rhetoric. Parents need encouragement and support in embracing their sacred vocation in raising "the greatest in the kingdom." They need to understand and be prepared for their role as "theologians in residence." They need to know that the communication of faith happens "in the midst" of the interactions and exchanges of everyday life—at the kitchen table, in the rocking chairs, through the witness of their own lives. Parents need to understand that seemingly ordinary actions are charged with meaning and possibilities. They need to believe that they can transform the mundane into the miraculous by awakening to the Divine Presence in the ordinary. All parents, not only a select few, need to feel capable of this transforming power—from parents in Covenant House to parents on Park Avenue.

The task of church ministers is not to do the job of religious education *for* the parents, but to do it *with* them and, most of all, to enable them to do the job themselves.

In the Archdiocese of New York, we begin our "up the river" ministry on the parish level when parents are expecting a child through birth or adoption with a Mass for Expectant Families. All of the services—a blend of spiritual, educational, social components that take place on the grassroots—are well designed, comprehensive, and tailored to the needs of the individual parish. They have an umbrella title of "Bringing Families Together." The overarching goals are (1) to bring individuals in families closer together in Christian love; (2) to bring parish families together in community—building up the Body of Christ; (3) to bring estranged families back to the life of the Church.

The response of parents has been overwhelmingly enthusiastic and grateful. Many parents have commented that the only time the Church paid attention to them was at points of sacramental preparation for their children, which was generally in the form of mandated meetings. Between the sacraments, they say they felt ignored. Fortunately, our ministry to parents "between the sacraments" has changed this perception and so many are now returning to the Church or becoming more involved in the Church because they perceive the Church as truly caring about them.

One of the most important lessons that has been learned through this ministry is that if parents are going to be reached and subsequently change, then key systems in the parish that have an impact on the family—such as the school, catechectical program, youth ministry program—must also change.

For decades, the delegation model of education has existed: "Give us your children and we will teach them for you." This model is deeply embedded in the minds of many ministers and parents. Therefore, turf problems erupt between parents and professionals. To move toward a partnership model requires education. Hence, all those key people—priests, educators, catechists—who work in the systems that support the family must be prepared to minister collaboratively with parents. Consequently, training programs in seminaries, colleges, universities, and certification programs must include a parent education ministry component. All systems need to be working together to transform the Church and society in Christ.

In creating the symbols for the word *crisis*, the Chinese were quite insightful. Danger exists, but opportunities abound. We need to dream and move beyond the way the world is, to the way we would like it to be. We need a "mindscape." With the passion of the Holy Spirit and energy only the love of Christ can provide, together in Jesus' name, we can transform the world. The dream is big; the place it begins is small—in the family!

Suggested Reading

Amendolara, Lorraine P. *Establishing Parish Parenting Centers*. Huntington, Ind.: Our Sunday Visitor, 1990.

_____. and Mary Longo. *Good Beginnings* (A Parent Education Curriculum). Huntington, Ind.: Our Sunday Visitor, 1990.

_____. *Growing Up Together* (A Parent Education Curriculum). Huntington, Ind.: Our Sunday Visitor, 1990.

_____. *Parents and Teens Together* (A Parent Education Curriculum). Huntington, Ind.: Our Sunday Visitor, 1990.

Amendolara, Lorraine P. and Eileen Murphy. *Communicating Christian Sexuality to Children* (A Parent Education Curriculum). Huntington, Ind.: Our Sunday Visitor, 1990.

Barber, Lucie W. *The Religious Education of Pre-School Children*. Birmingham, Ala.: Religious Education Press, Inc., 1981.

Durka, Gloria and Joan Marie Smith, eds. *Family Ministry*. Minneapolis, Minn.: Winston Press, 1980.

Fowler, James W. *Stages of Faith*. New York: Harper and Row, 1981.

Greeley, Andrew M. *The Religious Imagination*. New York: Sadlier, 1981.

John Paul II. *Familiaris Consortio*. Washington, D.C.: USCC Office for Publishing and Promotion Services, 1981.

_____. *On Catechesis in Our Time*. Washington, D.C.: USCC Office for Publishing and Promotion Services, 1979.

Lynch, Thomas. "What Is the Method in Today's Family Madness?" *Momentum* (September 1987).

National Conference of Catholic Bishops. *A Family Perspective in Church and Society*. Washington, D.C.: USCC Office for Publishing and Promotion Services, 1988.

United States Catholic Conference. *Sharing the Light of Faith: National Catechetical Directory for Catholics of the United States*. Washington, D.C.: USCC Office for Publishing and Promotion Services, 1979.

Notes

1. Thomas Lynch, "What Is the Method in Today's Family Madness?" *Momentum* (September 1987): 23.

2. James W. Fowler, *Stages of Faith* (New York: Harper and Row, 1981), pp. 119-120.

3. Andrew M. Greeley, *The Religious Imagination* (New York: Sadlier, 1981), p. 61.

4. Lucie W. Barber, *The Religious Education of Pre-School Children* (Birmingham, Ala.: Religious Education Press, 1981), pp. 14-15.

Awakening Religious Imagination and Creativity

by Judy Gattis Smith

> The chilling fact for us as parents and teachers is that while we cannot give a child creativity (it is his or her unique right), we can take it away. While we cannot birth it in another, we can kill it.

Foreword

Though the words *imagination* and *creativity* are sometimes used interchangeably, to my mind there is a distinction. In using the word *imagination* in this article we will be talking about revelation, visions, and dreams and how to recognize and cultivate these manifestations. *Creativity* to me suggests innovative approaches and the word is used in that context here.

Imagination

The story is told of a very young boy and his father who were attending Mass together. The service had not progressed very far when the father felt an insistent tugging on his coat sleeve.

"Father! Father!" the young boy said in as much of a whisper as a child can muster. "Why is God wearing a green suit today?" The father gave the boy the frowning countenance he thought the question deserved, but the boy continued: "Father, why is God wearing a green suit today?" The father looked now at the son and saw not a flippant or silly expression on his face but one of deep reverence and awe. Seeking a logical explanation, the father asked, "Where?" "There!" the boy said. "Just above the candles."

Judy Gattis Smith, Christian educator and author, emphasizes a creative and sensory approach to religious education. She lives in Lynchburg, Virginia.

The father looked back and forth between the rapturous expression on the child's face and the emptiness he saw behind the candles. Finally he replied, "I don't know, son."

Many times we are tempted, as adults, to look at great things and see nothing and then deny that anything can be seen. Because our path to visions and dreams is blocked, we deny that a path is there at all.

Visionary imagination can be a powerful force in young children and we are sometimes afraid or embarrassed by its presence. If we recognize it at all, we hasten to label it as simplistic.

Our problem as parents and teachers is not so much how to awaken the spiritual imagination of a child, but rather how to nurture it. Our task is threefold: (1) how to affirm it; (2) how to give children words and stories to name it; and (3) how to devise methods to express it.

Affirmation

We begin with affirmation. How many of us saw visions as a child—times when our eyes were opened to the very presence of God—times when we were enveloped in a numinous reality—times that remain with us all our lives, and once known, cannot be unknown?

Yet, even at an early age, in the intuitive way that children have of reading adults, we knew that this was something not to be expressed.

The spiritual imagination of a child is a delicate thing, a tiny wood violet in the spring. We so easily crush it beneath our heavy heels. We do this in two ways. One, by our expressions and lack of attention we discount its importance. Two, we rush forward too quickly to explain it—to explain it—to coat it with pious explanations. Children ask questions out of their religious imaginations. We need to tune our ears very finely to pick up these overtones.

When my granddaughter, Sarah Neel, was four she was intrigued with using the telephone and searched for any excuse to call her grandmother. One day the phone rang and I heard a little voice say: "Grandmother, the tulips are blooming!" "How wonderful!" I replied. "Did you plant them?" (I knew she had.) "Yes," she said eagerly. Then, after a pause she added, "But I don't know who made the blossom."

Spiritual imagination is closely aligned to wonder and here is the world where children often feel more at home than we do. It is their environment and they are often the teachers, not us. A church school teacher shared with me a moment of spiritual awakening for her. She was reading the story of one of Jesus' healings to a group of five-year-olds. Imprinted on her mind forever, she said, is the expression of a little boy who was hearing this story for the first time.

"Do you mean," he asked with intensity, "that Jesus just *touched* him and he was well? Wow! That Jesus! Wow!"

Albert Einstein is reported to have said: "The fairest thing we can experience is the mysterious. He who knows it not, who can no longer wonder, can no longer feel amazement, is as good as dead or a snuffed-out candle."

We open our children to God as we affirm and encourage wonder. Dr. Robert Coles, Pulitzer prize author and chronicler of children's behavior, said in an interview reported in *Newsweek* magazine, December 10, 1990:

Now many children are ashamed of their spirituality, afraid of being mocked by the secular community, afraid that others will see them as absurd, foolish or superstitious. It is another instance when what's happening in children's lives accurately reflects what's happening in the adult world.

As parents and teachers, this then becomes our first task, to attune ourselves to the voices of children—to hear, behind the obvious questions they ask, the spiritual overtones—to humble ourselves so that we may learn from them how to travel the road of wonder—to affirm as valid a child's different definitions and dimensions of knowing God—to affirm their visions and dreams.

Words and Stories

Our next task is to give the children words and stories to express their imaginations.

Have you ever listened to two musicians talking together about a piece of music? Heads bent over the manuscript, they struggle for words to express their feelings. Hands fluttering, they sputter, "Here's the build-up." "See here? What is the composer saying?" Foreheads pucker as they struggle to communicate. Then words like *crescendo, adenza, vivace* come to their rescue. They escape into a private language that communicates what everyday, getting-the-job-done words do not.

We feel some of the same struggle to communicate—to take things from one level of reality to another as we read some of the visionary experiences in the Bible. For example, read Daniel, chapter 8. The author is hard-pressed to explain the revelation he experienced. He struggles to find images to express a truth that reason cannot penetrate.

But following this, we read in Daniel 10:1:

> In the third year of King Cyrus of Persia, a *word* was revealed to Daniel who was named Balachazzar. The *word* was true and it concerned a great conflict. He understood the *word* having received understanding in the vision.

First comes the imaginary vision, seeing in the mind's eye, the truth of God. After the experience of a vision comes a means to communicate it—a word.

Given a word we can make some kind of jump—a connection. In his book *The Grace of Great Things*, Robert Grudin says, "The most powerful single symbol yet produced by humanity is '=' (the equal sign)." This suggests the translation of an experience from one type of signification to another and by extension the translating power of the mind.

First the vision, the inspiring impulse, then the shaping principle of a word. We can give our children a religious vocabulary—sacred words—as the other side of the "=," a symmetry between the vision and the expression of it.

Spiritual imagination is closely aligned to wonder, and here is the world where children often feel more at home than we do.

What a young child perceives about God is at least partially inaccessible to adults, yet we are seeking here to ensnare the dreams and visions in the airy net of words and signs.

When Jesus' disciples were struggling to understand the power and the peace that came to Jesus when he prayed, they implored him, "Teach us to pray." Jesus gave them words, our Lord's Prayer, that they might verbalize the experience that is the environment of visions.

In the same way, we as teacher and parents can give a vocabulary to our children to help them express and communicate those experiences of spiritual imagination. We can reclaim those words with long religious traditions and reanoint them to be our vehicles to carry us into the realm of spiritual imagination. Sacred words incorporate our rich religious traditions and heritage.

For example, consider words like *hallelujah*. What a rich history this word has in the Eastern world, going back to the high trill of the tongues (the "hallel") used to express extreme joy. We heard examples of this from our television sets as the women of Kuwait welcomed the liberating forces into their cities. It was intense joy, needing a special sound to communicate it.

There are many other words in our spiritual vocabulary. We can hold sacred these words: *Amen; Gloria; Shalom; apostle; covenant; discipleship; heaven; angels; rapture; bliss; paradise; Eden; Calvary; blessed; saints; worship; prayer; grace; Hosanna; Pax.* You may think of others. These words bring forth vital operating power and connotation.

We can give our children "picture-words" that help them understand who we believe Jesus was and God is: *I am the Door; I am the Good Shepherd; I am the Way; I am the Bread of Life; I am the Light of the World.*

Drawing on religious language becomes an act of disclosure. Words may help give shape to the children's visions. In addition, we can teach children the great stories of our faith as background for their spiritual experiences. Sacred dreams are our inheritance.

God comes, in wonder and joy, whenever and wherever God wills. From our biblical heritage we learn that God's ways are not our ways. Visions can be seen from burning bushes or great lights and smoke on the mountain. As we tell and retell these stories to our children, we affirm that they did happen and that they can happen again. Thus, we lay a groundwork, a foundation for a child's visions.

We realize that just as we affirm a football player *could* make a breakthrough in a great medical discovery, it is much more likely that a doctor would make this discovery. In the same way, God will be revealed where and when God chooses, but it seems more likely that God would appear to a person experienced in spiritual practices.

We cannot teach our children how to call God to us on demand, but we can prepare the way for God's coming.

So, our second task in nurturing spiritual imagination is to give our children sacred words to express their visions and sacred stories to serve as a foundation for understanding these visions, a context in which to place these extraordinary happenings. Plant within them the stories of Daniel and Ezekiel. Tell about Peter's vision on the rooftop and Paul's journey to Damascus. Marvel with them over Jacob's ladder to heaven and the multitude of angels who sang to the shepherds on the hillside. And say again and again, "And in such ways as these, God may speak to us again!"

Send them out from your classroom or home each day with these affirming words: "May you see the mystery of God today!"

Method of Expression

We affirm our children's visions. We give them a vocabulary to express them, aware that words can never fully capture the dream. Now, we seek to give them some way to embody these spiritually imaginative thoughts, visions and dreams—moving from feeling to thought to expression.

We don't know where children's ideas come from, and we need to be checking constantly to see what they understand.

An article in the newspaper in Lynchburg, Virginia, told about children who had misunderstood the meaning of the word *stranger*. When their parents had said, "Don't speak to a stranger," or "Don't let strangers into your house," they continued to speak to strangers and let strangers in their homes. Asked why, the children gave what was to them a logical explanation. One of the more unusual ones was, "He wasn't a stranger because he had a clipboard."

We need to clarify that the words and stories we have given children are understood, and we need something more than words to aid the communication between them and us.

In giving an outlet for expression of visions, we teachers and parents become more deliberate. We seek to provide some method to remove the shadowy screen and make communication possible. When we give children media as a concrete outlet for a dream or a vision, there should be: (1) no copying or imitation, or (2) no adult interference in the children's work. The children express their own experiences and visions and dreams.

Since we are dealing here with a different kind of expression, a different mold and cast of thought, we need different tools. Let's look at four specific methods: art, music, movement, and poetry.

Art. There is an almost endless variety of art media. I like aerosol shaving cream on a smooth table to give children an expressive media for dreams. Just put a glob on the table. Children, using their hands, illustrate their dream. There is the same fading-away, ethereal quality to this media as to dreams. I like other "feeling-touching" art media: clay; finger paints; touch collages. Water colors, pastel chalk, crayons, and paper are all good. The media should not be so difficult to master that the children get bogged down in technique.

We cannot teach our children how to call God to us on demand, but we can prepare the way for God's coming.

Music. Music, with its ability to touch another realm of reality, is a good outlet for dreams and visions. A wordless tune may express the feeling of a divine revelation. What a gift we give our children when we give them a musical skill in which they can express themselves. Unfortunately, this skill often takes years of specialized training. If this is impossible, a modern tool, the tape recorder, may come to our aid here. Encourage your child to go alone with a tape recorder and sing his or her song. Create with sudden tune or careless rhyme. Capture the fleeing impression in tones. A class can create a hymn together in the same way—a paeon of praise—an outburst of joy—an actual hearing of a numinous experience.

Movement. We can expose our children to great music that resonates to the deep undertones of life and then instruct them to use their bodies to sway and move to the music (Mozart's "Hallelujah," for example). In such a way, the children give physical expression to unworded pain or unexpressible happiness. Swaying, turning, arms uplifted, reaching to God. The body has power to communicate and often our bodies can say things our words cannot. The language of movement is powerful and memorable. Music on records or tape or live music played on different instruments could be helpful here. Prepare your child or class for this kind of expression at an early age.

Experience different kinds of walking. Walk to biblical illusions. How would you walk to see baby Jesus in the manger? How would little lambs walk following a good shepherd? How would you walk in the Palm Sunday parade? How did you walk to church this morning? What moving expresses your dream? Help your child feel comfortable using his or her body to communicate feelings.

Poetry. Poetry with its sudden seeing, its imagery, its freshly connected metaphors can give embodiment to dreams and visions. Encourage your child or class to express with only three or four lines, like *haiku* poetry, the essence of their dream or vision. I would not worry about spelling or line count or rhyming, however, but rather suggest that your child begin with a normal thing or general statement such as, "In my dream I saw. . . ." Then ask them to recall the strangest, most beautiful part of the dream. Ask them to put themselves in their dream. Feel as if you are in that place. Tell what you see and how it makes you feel, or tell about strange and wonderful beings who were there and what they did. Make up strange names to describe them or tell about a beautiful landscape you saw.

A child might capture the essence of a vision by repeating words. For example: "Shining, shining, shining!"

Concrete poems are poems where the words form the shape of the thing described. This is a good method for dream and vision poetry. For example, if there is the imagery of the sea, the child's poetry might be written across the page like waves. If the essence of the dream is vague and floaty, it could be described by writing words in the shape of clouds.

David Heller, in his book *The Children's God*, offers other suggestions for housing children's visions. He suggests naming, drawing, and storytelling about God, and writing letters to God.

Through these non-question/answer methods children reveal an abundance of imagery to us.

In addition to methods to express visions, we can help our children become comfortable with the silence in which these swift insightful dreams can grow. To give children the gift of listening for the Truth that seeks us, we teach them to quiet themselves, turn inward, wait, and listen.

Being outdoors, in close communion with nature, is an excellent beginning place for children to learn to listen to silence. Invite them to find a special place outdoors to sit alone. You might challenge them with suggestions such as: "Listen and try to hear the grass growing"; "Feel the sun on your back. What is the sun saying?"; "Pretend you are an empty balloon. What is filling you?"; "Find a large rock. Sit beside it and be a rock. Do everything the rock does."

As we parents and teachers seek to create a place where spiritual imagination is fed and the visions of God's reign are brightened, we should never underestimate the effect of praying, participating adults. Do not take lightly your part in God's plan of revelation through children. Your home or classroom is a setting where the numinous might appear, for anything and everything is capable of being flooded with the presence of divinity.

Remember: 1. Affirm your children's visions.
                    2. Give them words and stories to shape these visions.
                    3. Provide them with methods to express them.

Creativity

Move with me now to creativity. Teaching a child to be creative is an oxymoron. It's like saying: "teaching a baby to grow"; "teaching a bird to sing." Creativity is a natural development in children if we do not thwart it. Children see the world through fresh eyes. They make connections between dissimilar things. They bring their previous experiences together in a *now* moment and see something new. Is this not what creativity is?

A preschooler was asked to describe a piece of music the melody of which began on a low tone, moved up to a higher tone, and then descended to the original low tone. "It's like the letter A," she said.

A third-grader wrote about his visit to his grandmother's house. Here are a few of his insights: "You'd like my grandmother if you like the feel of jello. Her piano goes 'wang.'" He expressed a fresh clear way of looking.

We have all known a young child to discard an expensive gift and play with the box it came in. Children lean toward creativity.

Creativity reveals itself in a distinct way in the uniqueness of each individual. We marvel at a creator God when we realize that no two individuals are alike or express their creativity in exactly the same way. Creativity then is one's unique way of expressing one's self in the world.

The chilling fact for us as parents and teachers is that while we cannot *give* a child creativity (it is his or her unique right), we can take it away. While we cannot birth it in another, we can kill it.

A playful environment seems conducive to creativity—singing, music, dancing, and games open a child to creativity.

Creative expression is a seed in every person, but the ground must be tilled and watered and weeded. In what kind of ground does creativity best grow?

A playful environment seems conducive to creativity; singing and music, dancing, and games open a child to creativity. Why do we stop skipping? At what age? Reason and logic descend upon us like an iceberg and the spontaneous, creative response is frozen. Our task is one of thawing. Laugh and play with your child while discussing religion. Humor and creativity spring from the same source; seeing the analogy in a situation, making a jump between two divergent ideas. Creative impulses are released when we are free to play, to have fun, to lighten up. God created laughter and calls us to praise his name with dancing.

The second enriching environment for creativity is an environment of curiosity. Ask "what if . . .?" as you tell Bible stories. What if the boy had not shared his loaves and fishes? Would Jesus still have performed a miracle? What if we had no Sunday school, how would we learn about Jesus?

We are, by nature, inquisitive creatures. Encourage your child's curiosity. Ask: "Is there a new way you could do this? Is there a better way? Is there a way you could do it that is different from the way I could do it?"

Encouraging and enjoying the creative approaches your child suggests sets your child on the right path. In a free, playful atmosphere, prodded by curiosity, we have the grounds for innovative approaches.

But to be creative as an end in itself is not our purpose. We search for the creativity, the innovative approach, that will reveal the Love that is at the core of the universe and help us respond to that Love. To release a child to be creative we teach that creativity is not for personal control or self-enhancement. God is at work in your child's life and he or she should have a sense of that.

We may be able to cultivate the natural gift of creativity, but to what end?

I heard Mr. Rogers, of the television show "Mr. Rogers' Neighborhood," tell of visiting preschools so as to keep in touch with children's interests and concerns. At one preschool he noticed an unusual amount of interest in play dough. His curiosity aroused, he asked the teacher, "Why?" She explained that a sculptor lived down the street and often visited the preschool, bringing his tools with him. Her words: "He doesn't teach. He just loves the clay in the presence of the children, and they pick up on this and love to create with play dough."

As we adults seek to foster creativity, we invite the children to the Creator. In addition to fun and curiosity, we "love the clay" in the presence of the children and, exposed to this Love, they create.

Suggested Reading

Grudin, Robert. *The Grace of Great Things.* San Francisco: Ticknor and Fields, 1990.

Harris, Maria. *Teaching and Religious Imagination.* San Francisco: Harper and Row, 1987.

Heller, David. *The Children's God.* Chicago: University of Chicago Press, 1986.

Palmer, Parker. *To Know as We Are Known/A Spirituality of Education.* San Francisco: Harper and Row, 1983.

Smith, Judy Gattis. *Developing a Child's Spiritual Growth through Hearing, Seeing, Tasting, Touching and Smelling.* Nashville: Abingdon Press, 1983.

_____. *Teaching to Wonder.* Nashville: Abingdon Press, 1989.

_____. *Grandmother Time.* Dallas: Word Publishing, 1991.

Obeying the Mystery: Worship and the Very Young

by Mary Catherine Berglund

> If we do not keep in touch with the child within, if we have lost our sense of wonder and do not care to retrieve it, we will not worship effectively with children.

"When a mystery is too overpowering, one dare not disobey." Thus the child in the grown-up Saint-Exupery explained to himself the happy compulsion he felt to draw yet another sheep for the strange, small, demanding person who stood before him in the desert—a sheep not already very sickly, nor horned like a ram, nor too old to live a long time. So the downed pilot drew only a box with a few holes and announced that the little sheep his companion wanted was inside. And a light of contentment broke over the little prince's face. . . .

The Child Within

Often when I want to think about children—always when I want to think about children and God—I reread *The Little Prince*. Its perceptive author unfailingly leads me to deeper insight into the fleeting gifts of childhood and stirs within me a yearning for that sense of wonder which accompanies only poets into adulthood. The gentle Frenchman reminds me that the child in each of us still lives, however suppressed that child may be by the sophistications and practicalities of adulthood. If we do not keep in touch with the child within, if we have lost our sense of wonder and do not care to retrieve it, we will not worship effectively with children. Indeed, we will not worship effectively at all.

Mary Catherine Berglund writes and lectures on children's liturgy. Presently, she is a doctoral candidate at Union Theological Seminary in Richmond, Virginia.

Our objective in this chapter of our book is to reflect upon children and worship. How can we—parents and other adult guardians of children, leaders of liturgical gatherings, religious educators—enable the youngest members of our community to worship God authentically? How can we—years beyond childhood—join the very young in praise of God, that essential act of our beings that imitates, though ever so feebly, not only the heavenly, saintly chorus but also the glorious triune perichoresis? In our efforts to answer our questions, let us attend, though not neatly, first to the person we praise, then to the little ones whose praising engages our attention, and finally to reflection directly on worship with children.

A World of Symbol and Mystery

God lives in mystery far more than does the sleepy little sheep in the holy box. We cheat our spirits with our profound and pious pronouncements if we think they encompass God. Worship is unrestrained, joyful obedience to the mystery of God, not rational statements about God. Those liturgical gatherings are sterile which so consume our understanding that they do not admit that worship is bowing to mystery. Certainly, we cannot pray with the very young if we forget that God lies far beyond our deepest human endeavors.

Children go directly to God, resisting our learned talk. Extensive discourse on the primal power of light, for example, will not interest a young child, but the repeated lighting of a candle, accompanied by the simple, ancient proclamation, "Jesus Christ is the light of the world, light no darkness can put out," will forge in the child's psyche an unbreakable linking of Jesus and light—Jesus, in whose presence all created light is only darkness.

Long before we begin to explain to the very young the things of God, we introduce them to symbol and simple ritual: we light candles in their presence; we sign them with the cross; we sprinkle them with water; we anoint them with oil; we let incense float in the air around them; we dress them in white; we include them in our meals, breaking bread with them and giving them sips of wine from our cups; we embrace them in loving forgiveness and earnest apology. These ritual acts ought to begin at home so that children will grow comfortable with them, knowing them intimately, like their language, before they reflect consciously upon them.

The cyclic unfolding of the liturgical year provides rich opportunity to nurture even young children in the traditions of our worship. An Advent wreath as mealtime centerpiece, for example, serves as a reminder of the joyful anticipation of both comings of the Lord Jesus: his coming in mystery centuries ago and his coming in majesty not yet. A creche, even an inexpensive set of play-inviting figures, helps children incorporate the Christmas story into the fabric of their lives. A cross of twigs, supported in a simple dish of sand, makes appropriate Lenten decor. If the twigs come from a not-yet flowering bush and are properly woven to form the cross, and if the sand is kept wet, the cross will bloom. A transparent bowl of water is a powerful Eastertime reminder of our baptismal dying and rising with Christ. Adults and children can take turns sprinkling a group with water while the whole group sings the wider community "Alleluia." A bouquet of fire-colored helium-filled balloons marks Pentecost in the hearts of children as celebration of Spirit-wind and Spirit-fire. Time comes when our children hunger for explanations of our rituals. If our explanations then are of habits already part of their very beings, then our no-longer-so-little ones will receive our halting words in joy as nourishment for their spirits, and not merely as inadequate attempts to contain the essentially elusive.

The Sacred Stories

Story, like symbol and ritual and the little prince's box, conceals and reveals. Sacred story conceals and reveals consuming truth about the very God before whom we bend our knees, each story a perpetual invitation to enter more deeply into God's personal self-disclosure. Sacred story shapes the consciousness of our children as specifically Christian, even as it draws them into the community of faith and feeds their growth in the faith community's traditions. Our children should hear the stories of our faith from their earliest months, even as they hear the sagas and legends born through decades of millennia in our natural human culture. Parents and other guardians of children, of course, own the privilege of primary presence with our little ones. They bear their personal and community responsibility well by reading our Bible stories to their children and by giving them their own age-appropriate Bibles with pictures to look at and image further; eventually, the children may read the text themselves, think deeply about it, and act upon it.

The parish community can assist these bearers of the bearers of our future by offering continual, quality, multilevel adult scripture study. The parish serious about passing on its faith story will also provide regular word-based children's programs. To assist this endeavor, the parish might enlist generous teens and other folk not burdened with all-consuming daily responsibilities to attend the parish nursery specifically to read Bible stories to small groups of very young children. The parish might also organize occasional Bible-centered story- and song-fests or Bible art or drama camps. All Christians are diminished if we lack imagination and energy to lead children to engagement with our vast and vital biblical story from its opening magnificent liturgy of creation to its final immense liturgy of rapturous heavenly praise.

*To draw children into meaningful
participation in our liturgy of
the eucharist is a challenge
the Church at large has yet to meet.*

God is really the God of biblical revelation. Since the primary attestation of the biblical word is that God loves us, to convince children of God's love is our primary goal in introducing to them our Scriptures. There was a time when we could teach children that God loves us like a loving parent, like a caring mother or a tender father. In today's fractured, violent society, however, we must with sensitivity liken God's love to experiences wider than parental: God loves us also like a caring shepherd, like a faithful friend, like a pursuing lover, like a generous vine-grower, like an irked judge, like a poor woman, like a prodigal table-host.

Although we cannot claim for the Bible a function essentially different from its drawing of women and men of all ages into the circle of those who know God's love, we can express in other ways the significance of the Bible in the lives of the children who engage our attention. The Bible also offers children heroes and heroines to call forth their best abilities— superstars far more authentic than the jocks and the Hollywood queens and the heavy-metal studs who plaster the scandal sheets. The Bible can lead children to see the world through the eyes of the have-nots with the eyes of nascent liberation theologians. The Bible can induce children to ecstasy in company with the greatest mystics of history. Of course, we want to introduce our children to God through God's self-revealing word. Of course, we want our children to grow up with the stories of our faith.

Through the Eyes of a Child

Like the little prince and the unspoiled grown-up who meets him, young children exhibit two striking characteristics that assist us in our efforts to lead them into sacred story and symbol and ritual and, thus, into worship. The first is that children's sense of wonder is not yet jaded. Young children still take pleasure in simple things: soap bubbles, puddles, dandelions, butterflies and lightning bugs, piles of leaves, and piles of snow. Children glimpse God's presence and clap their hands and shout for joy. They hear first fresh words of God's love and respond with uncluttered trust. Children immediately identify themselves with the sheep whom the Lord pastures and protects. Children find genuine comfort in Jesus' words that God cares for us even more than for the flowers of the field and the birds of the air. Children understand the lady who cleaned her whole house to find one lost coin.

A second persistent characteristic of the very young that leads them naturally into worship is that they are prelogical in their reasoning processes. Children think differently from adults. They do not draw conclusions *obvious* to older persons. Clear analogies do not move them. Infallible argument does not convince them. Children have all kinds of questions, but their questions signal wonder, not doubt. Although such qualities are a decided handicap in older persons, in the very young they can be marvelous gifts. Adults, who understand so much, want to understand everything; but children are willing to stand unembarrassed before mystery. Adults all too often look upon the unexplained as weird, foolish, impossible; but children live in a world still bursting with miracles. What an advantage children have, then, when it comes to the mysteries of our faith! Children do not ask, "How can Jesus Christ have a divine nature and a human nature at the same time?" They just believe that Jesus, who is God, became a human person and lived with us. Children do not worry about how a woman can bear a child and still be a virgin. They just love Jesus' mother. Children do not puzzle over the medicinal powers of saliva. They just believe that Jesus healed the blind man by touching his eyes with his spit. Children do not say, "Oh, all the people there must have had food and shared it." They just believe that Jesus fed more than five thousand people with five loaves of bread and two fish. I do not belittle a probing, analytical, demanding, sophisticated adult faith; but how wonderful also when children of God believe with all their hearts without any hesitation at all!

Our Concept of Worship

As we consider the formative power of symbol and sacred story and ritual, it becomes clear that, unless we limit our concept of worship to its most formal expressions, we cannot effectively separate our preparation of children for worship and our worship with them. To tell our sacred stories, to enact in ritual the sacred experiences of our faith history, to identify the sacred moments in our personal lives with the sacred moments of our community life—worship is precisely such. It is not serendipitous, then, that our efforts to ready our children for worship are already informal worship with them. We wish, however, also to involve the very young in our formal community worship, and it is to this essential endeavor that we now attend.

We recognize, of course, that the very children who occupy the attention of the readers of this book are those children who are baptized but who have not yet received communion. These children have already participated in a most fundamental, most consequential formal liturgical experience: they have all been baptized into the Lord Jesus, into membership in our Christian community. We do not speak, then, of completely "unchurched" children, but we often fail to draw upon their privilege.

Children are like dancers: only in their movement are children deeply themselves.

Theologians have tried to express the power and the richness of baptism, but their efforts are feeble in comparison with the reality of the gift. The liturgy of baptism itself, however, proclaims loudly the effect of that first sacrament: baptized into the death of Christ and buried with him, we are washed free of sin and live now a new life. Baptism by immersion expresses most succinctly and most dramatically the metamorphosis the sacrament brings about. But the baptismal liturgy is even a veritable sensory feast accosting eye and ear and tongue and nose and skin, insisting that the sacrament touches every part of our beings. Even children can intuit the importance, though not the precise meaning, of such bodily involvement. We make it difficult for our children to appreciate their belonging to the Christian community if, after we baptize them, we do not continue to include them in the initiatory process. Children should be present frequently at the celebration of the sacrament to allow the liturgy both to foster their appreciation of their own privileged membership in the community of faith and to encourage their increasing responsible participation in community life.

One of the greatest benefits of the revised adult Christian initiation process is its restoration of the role of the community in the reception of new members. And even children can take part in the community action. They can, for example, voice a meaningful and enthusiastic "yes" to a simple questioning as to whether they are willing to live model Christian lives in order to give good example to others soon to join the company of persons, like themselves, who are already consecrated in Christ Jesus as a holy people. When their younger sister or brother is to be baptized, children can help design and decorate a white garment, symbol of baptismal grace, and a candle, symbol of the Lord Jesus in whose light we wish to walk until we take our places in the heavenly kingdom. Older children can have a voice in the weighty task of choosing for their baby sibling the name the child will bear forever, a happy, sacred task that might well involve research into both family and faith-community history.

By far the most significant formal worship experience of children is their participation in the community Sunday eucharistic liturgy. By its very nature, however, even in its simplified ancient-contemporary form, the eucharistic liturgy speaks primarily to adult Christians. The liturgy of the word, celebrating God's self-revelation to the human community, can be incomprehensible and tiresome to children (cf. *Directory for Masses with Children,* 2). The liturgy of the eucharist, celebrating God's gift of the Lord Jesus himself as our spiritual nourishment, is in most parishes so stylized an experience that the uninformed visitor can hardly recognize that we take part in a sacred meal. Furthermore, the community's exclusion of the very young from reception of the eucharist only intensifies in those impressionable young minds and hearts the strangeness of the professed meal.

All who work directly with the young and care about their spiritual development recognize the gravity of the problem. Even the Sacred Congregation for Divine Worship, in its remarkably sensitive *Directory for Masses with Children,* has expressed concern for the potential spiritual harm that accrues to children who are repeatedly subjected to liturgical experiences that not only do not touch them effectively but even, by their incomprehensibility, exclude them. We need not despair, however.

A Children's Liturgy of the Word

One liturgical adaptation that has had immense success in involving children in our Sunday eucharist is children's liturgy of the word. The primary focus is the celebration of a legitimate liturgy of the word for children as part of a regular parish Sunday celebration in which significant numbers of both children and adults comprise the assembly. After the opening prayer, the children leave the assembly for a separate gathering space in which adult leaders proclaim and explain, specifically for the children, one or several of the lectionary selections for the day. Meanwhile, the adult assembly celebrates its usual liturgy of the word, pleased by its appropriate incorporation of children into its worship. At the conclusion of both liturgies of the word, the children return to their parents or other adult guardians, and the entire assembly celebrates the liturgy of the eucharist together.

To preserve the advantages of this liturgical adapation, it is vital that all persons involved, children and adults alike, understand it as part of our Sunday liturgy and not, for example, as convenient critical-time baby-sitting or as lectionary-based religious education. The children's liturgy of the word extends to an essential segment of the worshiping assembly a proper and timely celebration of God's word and, at the same time, encourages the assembly to look upon itself as a united body of variously gifted Christians.

To present the ecclesiological and pedagogical advantages of a children's liturgy of the word, however, only begins to describe it fairly. It is a constant delight to children and adults alike. To watch children gather eagerly for their dismissal from the assembly and to see their happy faces as they rejoin the assembly are experiences alone sufficient to persuade parishioners that a liturgy of the word for children is beneficial. Those adults privileged actually to proclaim the word to children witness a constant joyful openness to God's word—a telling reaction perhaps more like the fresh response of the first Christians and less like the response of those jaded churchgoers who have heard the good news repeatedly and resist its difficult claims upon their lives. This adaptation also offers the community ready opportunity to include children in its special seasonal liturgical rites. For example, singing, palm-waving children, bound shortly for their liturgy of the word, may crowd around the presiding celebrant in the Passion Sunday entrance procession; banner- and streamer-bearing children, prepared during their special service of the word, may lead the assembly in a festive Christ the King recession.

The details of organizing and running a children's liturgy of the word may not be immediately evident, and those who are interested but apprehensive are encouraged to consult the suggested reading list at the conclusion of this essay for additional theoretical considerations and practical help. In addition, it would be beneficial to read the entire brief *Directory for Masses with Children,* which authorizes significant adaptation of our eucharistic liturgy for use with children.

To draw children into meaningful participation in our liturgy of the eucharist is a challenge the Church at large has yet to meet. Smaller, more intimate eucharistic gatherings would certainly help lessen the children's (in fact, the entire community's) feeling of distance from the center of our great eucharistic action, but a community will not have smaller gatherings without an adequate number of ordained leaders. The Catholic community will certainly not have smaller gatherings as long as it remains bound by a shortage of presiding celebrants, including those who know children intimately.

Even in large gatherings, however, there are certain practices that help draw children into the liturgy of the eucharist. Even toddlers can learn our responses and acclamations, unless, of course, our musical settings are esoteric—a not uncommon practice that often distresses much of the assembly anyway. Eucharistic ministers should acknowledge those youngsters not yet of eucharistic age who accompany adults as they come forward to share the sacred bread and cup. All the children in the nursery, even the babies, might join the assembly for its final blessing. An assembly with a fair proportion of children might learn to sing the appropriate acclamations and use, now and then, one of the eucharistic prayers for children, each of which invites a more animated participation on the part of the assembly than do the usual anaphoras.

A parish that ordinarily celebrates a children's liturgy of the word might provide an occasional, complete separate liturgy for children. The presence of a presiding celebrant who understands children and values their lively spirit is, of course, a rich asset for such an undertaking. Nonordained adult leaders may assist the presiding celebrant, even speaking to the children after the gospel as the *Directory for Masses with Children* proposes (see no. 24).

Providing children have met the requirements set forth by the Church for the reception of first communion, some may be lead more quickly into fuller participation in our eucharistic feast. The requirements for reception of eucharist, as formulated in the early years of the present century, are simple and reasonable: children should know something of the life of Jesus; children should know that there is a difference between ordinary bread and eucharistic bread; and children should want to receive the eucharist. Children from families who are conscious of God's presence and who attend Sunday liturgy regularly—especially a Sunday liturgy with a children's liturgy of the word—may well be ready for first communion before they are the usual seven or eight years old. Parishes might provide helpful pre-eucharist instruction for parents early in the lives of their children; keep in touch with these families; supply books for children and parents to use together when children show an interest in the sacrament; and, then, trust parents to make the decision concerning exactly when they will lead their children, with unrestrained joy, to the table of the Lord.

Conclusion

We have reflected, however incompletely, upon the nature of children and their capacity for worship, and we have considered specific ways of fostering their participation in our liturgy. Let me offer a concluding image of children, not from *The Little Prince* but perhaps faithful to its wisdom, an image of children that I often find helpful in planning their liturgical experiences. Children are like dancers: only in their movement are children deeply themselves. We may stop them occasionally and try to grasp their particularities, but in the very act of holding them still, we strip them of essential, precious attributes. We who wish to help children grow closer to God must respect their unique qualities, encouraging their natural dancing, even if we cannot join it with abandon. And we should not be surprised if we glimpse in that dancing a profound reflection of the God we worship, the God whose deepest reality consists not in static perfection but in dynamic creative relationship.

Suggested Reading

Berglund, Mary Catherine. *Gather the Children*. Vol. for Year B. Washington, D.C.: The Pastoral Press, 1993. This series originally printed in 1987, 1988, and 1989 is presently being revised to correlate with the new *Lectionary for Masses with Children*. Years C and A will be available soon. Includes extensive suggestions for leading Sunday and holy day liturgies of the word with children. Introduction presents theoretical and practical overview of the program.

Committee on the Liturgy, National Conference of Catholic Bishops. *Lectionary for Masses with Children*. Approved for use in the Dioceses of the United States of America by the National Conference of Catholic Bishops and confirmed by the Apostolic See. Chicago: Liturgy Training Publications, 1993. Offered in four volumes: Sundays of Years A, B, and C, and Weekdays. Presented in two formats: hardcover ritual edition for use in liturgical celebrations; softcover study edition for preparation of those celebrations. The study edition will be helpful to teachers, catechists, parents, clergy, principals, liturgists, musicians. Lectors, whether adults or children, may use this book to practice the readings.

De Saint-Exupery, Antoine. *The Little Prince*. Katherine Woods, trans. New York: Harcourt, Brace & World, 1943.

Nelson, Gertrud Mueller. *To Dance with God*. New York: Paulist Press, 1986. Offers insight into and suggestions for "family ritual and community celebration."

Sacred Congregation for Divine Worship. *Directory for Masses with Children*. Eng. trans. by the International Committee on English in the Liturgy. Washington, D.C.: USCC Office for Publishing and Promotion Services, 1973.

The Young Child and Scripture

by Jerome W. Berryman

If we wait to begin teaching children Scripture until they are in the third or fourth grade, we have missed the early years when children deeply absorb the bits and pieces of Scripture by their powerful sensitivity to language.

Scripture in the Home

In the beginning people experienced God, as we do today, as part of a web of relationships including the self, others, nature, and God. They could not explain what happened when they encountered God. All they could do was tell what happened. Stories about people who were especially close to God, like Abraham and Sarah, were told and retold.

The stories of God probably were told when families gathered around their fires at night. Children snuggled in among their parents and friends to listen. The stories wrapped the children in meaning and protected them like blankets against the cold and chaos of the night.

Later the stories were lettered by hand on scrolls. The spoken stories slowly became books. In the sixteenth century, the Scriptures began to be printed. The Great Story began to be heard again in the family circle, at least in the homes of the wealthy, but the story was read rather than told.

This is an important distinction to note in passing. Telling stories is a direct form of communication where the story comes out of the storyteller. Reading stories is also good for children, but the reading comes from the interaction of the book and the reader. This form of communication is not as direct and intense as storytelling.

Jerome W. Berryman is a noted author and a canon educator of Christ Church Cathedral, Houston, Texas.

Today, the Bible can be in every home. It is no longer expensive, but Scripture only can escape its print prison when its stories are read or told out loud.

The work of James Fowler[1] has provided empirical and theoretical emphasis on the importance of stories for the formation of faith. Stories are the primary way children put their world together and make sense out of their experiences.

Fowler has shown that young children understand narratives only in episodes at first. They focus on the bits and pieces of a story that are important to them. They cannot keep the whole structure "on hold." This is why they want to be told their favorite part of a story over and over again.

Sometimes as early as middle childhood when children begin to attend school, a more complex ability develops. During this second stage of story development, the child can coordinate a whole narrative—beginning, middle, and end. Following this step, a third stage of story interpretation and construction develops, sometimes as early as late childhood. At this stage, children begin to be able to combine several stories into a larger story.

If we wait until children are in the third or fourth grade to begin seriously teaching them Scripture, we have missed the early years when they deeply absorb the bits and pieces of Scripture by their powerful sensitivity to language. As this language is absorbed, it helps form the child's way of putting the world together. If we miss the early years, we miss grounding Scripture as the child's own family story.

What Are We to Do, Then?

Buy a big family Bible. Keep it in a special and visible place. When the stories are to be told or read, go get the Bible from its important place with an air of ceremony. Open it and keep it on your lap or nearby as you tell or read the stories from it. Whether the stories are read or told, the children need the closeness of the storytellers and the circle of safety against the cold and chaos of the night as part of the stories.

Of course, you don't read the Bible straight through. That is an adult task. Read the stories you like best. Your good feelings will make the words sing and give deep value to what is said. What is felt is more important than what is read. To teach the Bible you need to teach how much you love it.

Even if you read from Bible storybooks, make a production out of bringing your family Bible to the reading or telling place. You can tell the children that the story you are going to read or tell is from the Bible. It is a little book (or story) from the Big Book or Great Story. "Someone found it in the Bible," you might say. "They loved it so much that they made a little book (or story) about it, so they could keep it closer to them and carry it with them wherever they go."

You may think all of this is rather magical. It is. This is the way value is assigned by young children. It is only dangerous and restrictive if we keep the children at this level of cognition when they grow beyond early childhood.

It is also important to note that the magical stage of cognition brings with it a power as well as a limitation. Children have an unconscious way of learning languages that we adults can only stand in awe of. This is mentioned out of respect for the abilities of young children, but it also is mentioned to remind us again that Scripture needs to be part of the language children are absorbing if it is to be deeply held and valued as a way to make meaning.

The home is not the only place children can encounter Scripture. They also run into it in church, but the experience is not always a good one. We turn to that experience now.

God's House of Stories

The church building is the sensorial embodiment of the Christian journey. It is God's house of stories and traditions. They are worked into the wood, glass, metal, leather, cloth, and the shape of the building itself. Like the illiterate adults of the Middle Ages, children learn from those images.

Children also hear Scripture in church, but the adults who read Scripture in church sometimes use a strange, "stained glass" voice. The children are also far away from the reader, who is usually a stranger. What is read does not sound like a story even when it is.

To discover the child's view of church, move around the interior space on your knees. This is both a prayer and an effort to get to the eye level of the child. You will discover how hard it is for children to see much more than the back of the pew in front of them, or perhaps the backs of a few heads. The ceiling is an option, but if you look at it for very long your neck begins to hurt. Besides, someone will probably glare at you if you are a child. (Adults seem to be able to get away with all sorts of "misbehavior" in church that children are excluded from doing.)

One way to bring the house of stories into focus is to tell stories about what children see in the church. Someone needs to sit on the sanctuary steps to identify, name, and value the images and stories embedded in God's house. Why are there three steps? Why do we share the holy bread and wine? Why is there an eagle with a Bible on its back? What are the stories of the windows and carvings? Where did our church get its name? How did this place come to be built where it is? Where did it get its shape? There is much to tell and show. Sit on the sanctuary steps, look around, and dream like a child to discover what is there.

Buy a big family Bible. Keep it in a special and visible place.

Children also need to come with their parents to take walks around the church when worship is not in process. They need to wonder together about such things as the colors and kinds of the vestments. They can ask together how the table is prepared for eucharist. The parents and children can come close to the baptismal font and wonder why it is where it is in the church and why it has the shape it does. The parents can show the children how to understand and love their church.

Parents also need to support each other, to learn the stories, and become comfortable in the church with their children. Perhaps, someone even needs to model how to be with children in church. Parents need to know about patience and firmness, the importance of a sense of humor, and when it is time to take a break outside.

The clergy have a powerful opportunity to value children during their homilies. I don't mean by preaching about children. That is important, but what is even more important is to stop in mid-homily and enjoy the presence of children being there when a "disturbance" occurs.

The preacher might stop and say, "Children belong here. They are part of this family. They are also our future, and as our Lord said, they are even parables. Children are parables about how to enter the kingdom. We need to honor, respect, and ponder children in our church, so we can discover the true direction for our own journey."

When we move from worship to worship-education, it is only a matter of emphasis. The sacraments and preaching are in the church and the community gathers there for worship. Children learn much from taking part in worship, but placing them in a more intentional and appropriate environment can help them learn even more about communication with and about God.

The need for more careful teaching about how the whole system of religious communication works today is critical. This is because worship is a form of communication that has very little in common with the electronic messages we receive from our television sets.

Connecting Worship and Education

At the turn of the century in Italy, a young physician was experimenting with how to educate handicapped children. She converted the concepts she wanted to teach into sensorial materials. For example, she gave children wooden letters with sandpaper on them. They moved their fingers over the sandpaper because it felt good, while their muscle coordination for writing the letters was being prepared.

This person was Maria Montessori (1870-1952). She became so interested in education after the opening of her first school in 1907 that she resigned her medical and academic appointments in Rome in 1910 at the age of forty and began to devote full time to education. Her schools were all over the world by the time of her death forty-two years later.

What is surprising to many is that Maria Montessori was very interested in religious education. In 1916, she and her colleagues established an education and teacher-training center in Barcelona, Spain. During the next twenty years, she developed most of her advanced elementary school materials and theory there. Montessori also began to experiment in a systematic way with religious education. She said that this gave the "Montessori method a long-sought opportunity of penetrating deeper into the life of the child's soul and of thus fulfilling its true educational mission."[2]

Montessori's approach to education included a special emphasis on the environment and sensorial learning materials. She made sure that children had the freedom to make constructive choices about their learning tasks. Lessons were organized so children

54

could control their own errors, which gave additional emphasis to their constructive self-motivation. Respect for others and each other's work is a fundamental value in the Montessori community of children.

Among Montessori's students was an English Quaker born of missionary parents in Madagascar. E. M. Standing was educated in England and became a follower of Montessori. His biography *Maria Montessori: Her Life and Work*[3] is still read. He was a second-generation student of Montessori's approach to religious education.

In 1954, the leading third-generation student of Montessori's approach to religious education, Sofia Cavalletti,[4] began her work in Rome. She and her colleague, Gianna Gobbi, who knew Maria Montessori herself, have greatly expanded Montessori's earlier experiments in religious education. Cavalletti's broad interest in theology and her advanced training in the literature and languages of the Bible have given a sound and deep foundation in Scripture to Montessori's earlier experiments.

I, author of this chapter, completed my first degree in theology in 1962 at Princeton Theological Seminary. My original training in Montessori education was completed in 1972 in Bergamo, Italy at the International Center for Advanced Montessori Studies. It was during that year that I first met Sofia Cavalletti and began experimenting with this tradition of religious education. My recent publication, *Godly Play*,[5] is the fruit of some twenty years' experience working with children, following this method. It gives a fourth-generation view of what Montessori began almost a hundred years ago.

Scripture and Godly Play
The Quality of Relationships

When one reads or tells Scripture to young children, the quality and structure of the communication are very important. Value is assigned and meaning enhanced or minimized by how Scripture is communicated as much as by the content of Scripture itself.

Modern research has come to recognize what Montessori emphasized at the turn of the century about communication with children. The child's work is to grow, and the means for this growth is the senses. If you want to meet the child's deepest need to grow, then you need to play with the child in a sensorial way. Such play is the child's "work," which is to become a mature adult.

In the late 1970s, over twenty research-oriented books in English were published about play. This was twice the number of such volumes in the preceding fifty years![6] Today, we understand much more about play than we did in the past, so we are now in a position to describe more clearly how play can help us communicate Scripture to the young child.

Play is important because play makes human beings deeply happy. Researchers such as Garvey[7] have traced the natural history of the smile and laughter in relation to play. Koestler[8] discussed the spontaneous mirth that emerges in the creative act. Maslow concluded that playing and creating are necessary for human health.[9] These studies illustrate how creativity, a playful relationship with the environment, and the deep satisfaction of growth all bear positively on human identity and well-being.

One of the fundamental functions of narrative is to sustain and/or work out one's identity. Story provides the structure and the content of identity. Play is the spirit and the process by which identity can be sustained, discovered, and transformed.

There is another way to say this. We can say that human creatures are created in the image of God. We are all called to be creators by our very nature. We are called to play from our birth.

The image of Holy Wisdom playing with God at the beginning of creation has been loved by Jews and Christians alike for thousands of years. Wisdom is connected with the process of creation itself. Wisdom was there when God "established the heavens" and "laid the foundations of the earth." To paraphrase the poet who wrote of Wisdom in Proverbs, chapter 8:

> Then I was beside God as craftsperson,
> I was God's delight day by day,
> playing before God all the while,
> playing on the surface of the earth,
> and I found delight in the children.[10]

Play is a very powerful act. When children play "mommies and daddies," they become mommies and daddies. Piaget[11] called this an over-accommodation, a kind of play associated with imitation. He also noticed the over-assimilation aspect of play. When children play with an object such as a matchbox, it becomes for them the car or the baby carriage imagined. Perhaps, you can remember this from your own childhood.

Howard Gardner's studies of the child's use of metaphor and

language found play at work in language learning.[12] Preschool children often misunderstand metaphors, but they also use them with delight. They learn about language by experimenting with it playfully. This must be as true for religious language as it is for any other language domain of life.

> *To teach the Bible to children, you need*
> *to teach how much you love it.*

The most striking use of metaphors is found in the earliest years. There is a decline of the use of spontaneous metaphor during the elementary school years. Gardner concluded that the child has mastered his or her basic vocabulary by this time, so the need to be so inventive wanes. The school-age child also has a natural tendency toward conformity and rule-guided behavior. This discourages unsettling the categorical boundaries he or she just finished constructing.

In our culture, we tend to worship our work, which drives us to work at our play as an urgent and necessary reward. True play seems a waste of time. It is done for itself. When one truly plays, as children do, an indirect result is growth. When play is done as a reward or to gain some other end, it is no longer play. The ability of children to play is powerful.

The Pueblo Indians of northern New Mexico, for example, respect and value the power of children to play. This is because play can refresh adults and reawaken deep play within them, but there is another reason. Play enables children to make intuitive judgments about strangers. The elders make a point of asking the children if strangers are to be trusted.[13]

David Miller showed the broad influence of play in his book, *Gods and Games.*[14] He traced the study of play through anthropology, ethnology, sociology, economics, psychology, literature, philosophy, mathematics, and theology. In theology, he found discussions of play by Harvey Cox, Romano Guardini, Hugo Rahner, and other modern theologians as well as St. Thomas and Meister Eckhart in the Middle Ages. He also found that Nicholas of Cusa, Pascal, St. Augustine, Erasmus, Kierkegaard, and Clement of Alexandria were interested in the playfulness of religion and the metaphor of "the game" to define what theology does.

Theological play is not childish but child-like. It is for adults as well as children, but it is not about adults pretending to be children. It is in fact at the root of our Christian ethics. Hugo Rahner proposed that the ethic of the "grave-merry" person integrates classical humanism with the Christian sense of redemption.[15]

Play as a quality of communication is far from trivial. It is a state in which adults and children can truly join together without developmental differences getting in the way. One can meet the child in himself or herself in this way as well. It is also a way for humankind to be joined with the Creator, and to better know the earth. Play can lead one into a network of relationships where God, the earth, the self, and others can all be joined in one ultimate, delightful game.

Playing the "Ultimate Game" with Young Children

When we begin to be careful and intentional about worship-education, we need to have a clear structure to guide us and the children. We might name this educational structure most anything, but it is a game. It is a game to play, and it is a game worth playing. Deep play with Scripture draws us into the "Ultimate Game." Ordinary play becomes Godly play.

There are six aspects to any game: (1) the place for playing; (2) the pieces of value to play with; (3) the players; (4) the game's time; (5) the rules of the game; and (6) the game's goal. Let's take each of these aspects in turn to define further the activity of Godly play.

The Place of the Game

Young children can learn how to play the "Ultimate Game" by a carefully organized environment. The children are invited into a room where religious language physically surrounds them. When the content and structure of religious language has been made clear, the children can intuit a sense of the whole language system itself. They can identify, name, and value it from the inside, rather than as a distant observer of adult activities like in the church building or on a television screen.

The parables sitting in their boxes on the shelves of one section of the room can interact with materials from sacred stories in another part of the room. Lessons about baptism, eucharist, Advent, and other liturgical events also can be linked up with parables and sacred stories. The possibilities are endless and fruitful.

The primary learning that goes on in such a place is not "knowing one's biblical facts." It is the art of how to use the language to make meaning. The content of the language system is learned, but it is learned not as an end in itself. It is learned as a means to move toward God.

The Pieces of the Game

The "pieces" of religious language sitting on the shelves around the room are divided into the subfunctions of ritual, sacred story, and parable. This is helpful for the young children to notice as they work with the bits and pieces of the language system. They can notice this if the room is carefully arranged to disclose this pattern to them.

This is not unusual. We do the same sort of careful classifying when we teach mathematics. The learning, and sometimes the learning environment, is divided into the subfunctions of "putting together" (addition and multiplication), "taking apart" (substraction and division), and, perhaps, infinity.

Religious language also includes the powerful component of silence. This is a silence that comes not from outward control but from inner focus. It is not empty silence but full to overflowing. Such silence takes place when the shell of language is pierced by the child's natural meditation or when language is overwhelmed by the presence of God.

The wonder of parables opens the door to the mystery of God. The narrative of sacred story stimulates identity by locating one's personal story within the Great Story. The experience of liturgy stimulates the integration of one's use of action and gesture with Scripture to integrate one's whole being. Silence takes one beyond language.

The sensorial materials that embody Scripture follow a principle defined by Sofia Cavalletti. It is a process of clearing away all that is not "essential" to the image of language being presented.

The Players of the Game

The people in the worship-education center need to be looked at as a whole system of relationships. It is staggering to consider who else is involved in this teaching. God is present. The child's family and the larger church family have an influence on what goes on there. Even God's creation itself takes part in establishing the meaning that makes up the web of home in the larger world.

When something happens in any part of this vast system, the whole network of relationships is influenced. The adult guide in the classroom may never see the result of an intervention, but he or she needs to be aware of the potential power of such a move in the "Ultimate Game."

The Time of the Game

The passing of time is marked in the game by the rhythm of the holy eucharist. There is an opening, the giving of the lesson, the sharing of a feast and prayers, and a closing with something like a blessing. This rhythm has been chosen because people have communicated with God in community in this way since the beginning of the Christian tradition. This integrated pattern of actions defines the flow of time and experience so that the completeness of the experience gives time its meaning rather than vice versa.

This is not a kind of time kept by clocks. It is significant time that is important in this learning process. Clock time, however, needs to be managed carefully to enable the children to discover and value the significant time in which they meet God.

When one is "in Christ," one dwells in unique time. Past and future are drawn into the present and ordinary perceptions of time spread out into infinity.

Children naturally live in the present, but they need to become more conscious of that and value such experience, for it is only in the present that we can experience the presence of God. The past holds only borrowed, secondary experiences, and the future holds only hope. Sacred story develops along a line of time. There is a beginning, a middle, and an end. The liturgical function of relig-ious language is circular. The old year ends, and we begin to prepare again in Advent for the Nativity. The birth of Jesus ends on the cross, which is the beginning of Easter. The appearances come to an end at the Ascension, and the Church is born in

Pentecost. Parables create their own world where significant, unique time is the "normal" time of day.

The Rules of the Game

The rules of the game guide the players toward being more open to the goal. Teachers help keep the rules clear by example and by shaping the community of children to help each other keep the rules alive and positive.

One adult guide sits by the doorway to greet the children as they come in. This helps young children enter the room and separate from their parents in a relaxed and respectful way. The other guide, the storyteller, sits on the floor and helps the children find their place in the circle of the community of children. When all are ready, the storyteller presents a parable, a sacred story, or a liturgical act for the children to respond to.

The materials that make up a lesson are a translation from the print medium into one that connects with most all of the senses. The material, such as a parable in a golden box, is set in the center of the circle, which shows how Scripture is open to all as a way to make personal meaning. The teacher and the children come to Scripture equally, as children of God, to search out the depths of God together.

The adult guide does not "teach" in the sense of transferring an idea from his or her head into the head of the child. Instead, the teacher models how to enter Scripture and encounter God's mystery suspended there in its images. This art, like many arts, is taught by showing how and encouraging, rather than by telling how and forcing.

The materials are not used for free play, because Scripture needs to remain Scripture. The freedom and creativity occur in the response to Scripture. A response might be wondering together with the other children in the circle or in some art medium during the work period that follows.

After the presentation and wondering about the lesson in the circle, the children are dismissed from the circle, one at a time. The adult guide helps each child move with intention to his or her work. Some children will work on projects already begun during previous visits to the center. Others will create some new response in clay, paints, or some other medium. Some will go to the shelves and get out other material, such as the Exodus, to give themselves a lesson or to work in a group. Children are free to get other lessons. The only rule about getting materials off the shelf is that the child needs to have already had the presentation of the lesson. Either the storyteller or another child can show them.

The next step is for the children to put away their work and return to the circle for their feast. This is a time to share prayers, food, and drink together. It becomes an indirect preparation for eucharist.

The last step in the game is the dismissal. The storyteller tells each of the children good-bye, one at a time, when they come up to him or her before leaving the circle to go to the doorway. This is a moment to remind each child how wonderful it was to have him or her there that day. This is like a blessing.

Sometimes, television "families" become more familiar to a child than his or her own family. The child may spend a great deal more time with electronic families than human ones.

As you can see, the two adults in the room work together as guides to shape the community of children to work together to discover meaning for their lives in religious language. Both roles are very important. The storyteller needs the person by the door to be there in case someone who is unable to "get ready" needs to go and sit by him or her during the lesson.

The person by the door also helps when the children have trouble getting out their work. The storyteller remains seated in the circle to anchor that part of the process. After the work period, the person by the door also helps the children serve the napkins, cookies, and juice of the feast. This is a true collaboration among the two adults and the children.

The two adults in the room also work together to "disappear" as much as possible. This allows the children to sense more clearly the community of children. An "overadulted" setting discourages self-direction and the awareness of what St. Augustine called the "Inner Teacher."

"Disappearing" is done in various ways, such as sitting on the floor, moving on one's knees, or sitting in low chairs at the eye level of the children. Speaking slowly, softly, with clear intention, and with an economy of words also helps the children "do it themselves."

The six aspects of the "Ultimate Game" help us to remember who we are and what our goal is, as we guide the little ones. We turn to that goal now.

The Goal of the Game

The "Ultimate Game's" goal is to be open to experience the presence of the mystery of God. One might do everything right as a teacher and accomplish all of the objectives (the rules of the game) and still not meet this "elusive" goal. One can only play the game for the playing itself. God's presence cannot be forced, for we cannot control God.

Godly play is not like teaching math or geography. One must approach God indirectly through Scripture, trust the powerful language to do its job, and allow the whole network of relationships among the self, others, God, and the earth to do their work. These relationships are all connected, so deepening that one of these relationships stimulated all of them to move us all, including young children, toward ultimate meaning.

The Challenge of the Electronic Bible

We need a powerful and intentional way to teach Scripture to children while they are still young, because many of the deep language structures and fundamental values of children are formed before they are initiated into the print world of books and reading.[16] Television is often the young child's primary storyteller. However, television as a vehicle for telling stories defines the *content* of reality and, in its electronic way, shows the young child *how* to relate to and express what it has defined.

When television is used to introduce young children to Bible stories, it often drains the stories of their power. If we do not become more aware of how television presents Scripture and begin to act now, the voice of Scripture may be silenced or, at least greatly changed, in this generation by the electronic storyteller.

The electronic Bible[17] first appeared in 1949 with ABC's prime-time national religious television series, "I Believe." The electronic Bible has its own special way of communication. What is not successful in the marketplace of ratings and money disappears from the screen. Television must narrow down Scripture to what sells. What people need to hear from Scripture is often not what they want to hear, so the electronic Bible is a deeply compromised version of the original.

The television tube as a storyteller is confusing for children. It has a human voice, movement takes place on its screen, but despite the movement and human voice the box is not completely alive. Nevertheless, it has great authority. Adults sometimes even refuse to respond to other human beings in the same room when the television is speaking.

The story of electronic reality is authoritative, but the electronic "speaker" has never experienced God! This means that the nonverbal communication from it makes clear that God-talk and the experience of God need not be connected.

The television can undermine the child's trust of his or her own theological experience. It suggests to the child that a second-hand or hearsay knowledge of God, especially an electronic knowledge, will do. Reality breaks into two pieces for the child: electronic and existential reality compete for the child's full attention. The direct source of wholeness as the experience of God, self, others, and the earth is obscured by this fracture.

Sometimes, television directs its Bible-beam right at the children. Most children's programs on video turn the Bible into animated cartoons. This makes the Bible a frantic, busy, silly entertainment. Children absorb such nonsense uncritically and learn that the Bible is not related to the presence of God. It is not the Great Story. It is only trivial and cute. It is nonsense.

The living God responds to each human being's individual uniqueness and situation. Television has no such flexibility. Human beings of all ages must conform to its medium rather than meet God in its message. The electronic storyteller is shaping the identity of young children to be passive receptors rather than people born to create in the image of God, the Creator.

Television also can falsely satisfy the sacramental and community needs of children. It provides a ritual of programming to mark the passing of time for families. This ritual has no relation to genuine human needs and life process. It degrades them.

Sometimes, television "families" become more familiar to a child than his or her own family. The child may spend a great deal more time with electronic families than with human ones. If we add video games and electronic music to this equation, the balance tips badly toward the electronic definition of reality.

If church is encountered on television, it is probably an exciting and active view through the video window. Electronic church keeps one tuned in for a time, but the relationship is limited to the role of an observer. This kind of church can be very lonely. Finally, the flat church on the screen becomes irrelevant and teaches the child to identify, name, and value all church as irrelevant.

Television saps the energy it takes for children and adults to venture into the wilderness of their own lives to find the living God. We and the children wind up watching electronic pilgrims make the journey, if God is sought at all.

Most "religious education" today is carried on by the electronic Bible, whether we mean for it to be done that way or not. The tale that is being told, I am sorry to say, is not a Christian one. It is not even a useful one. That is why authentic and deeply felt storytelling to young children is so important at this moment in history.

Television is good for many things in this life, but it is not a good way to show young children the reality and language of "the elusive presence"[18] of God. When children experience God's presence directly and can identify, name, and value it, their interest in the artificial or secondhand experience of television will fade, and the Great Story will be heard and told again by a new generation.

Notes

1. James W. Fowler, *Stages of Faith: The Psychology of Human Development and the Quest for Meaning* (San Francisco: Harper and Row, 1981).

2. Maria Montessori, *The Child in the Church*, E. M. Standing, ed. (St. Paul, Minn.: Catechetical Guild, 1965), p. 23. A modern introduction to Montessori teaching that gives due respect to empirical studies as well as history is John Chattin McNichols, *The Montessori Controversy* (Albany, New York: Delmar Publishers, Inc., 1992).

3. E. M. Standing, *Maria Montessori: Her Life and Work* (New York: New American Library, Plume Book, 1984). Original Eng. trans., Hollis and Carter Ltd., 1957.

4. Sofia Cavalletti, *The Religious Potential of the Child* Patricia M. Coulter and Julie M. Coulter, trans.; preface by Mark Searle (Chicago: Liturgy Training Publications, 1992).

5. Jerome W. Berryman, *Godly Play: A Way of Religious Education* (San Francisco: Harper San Francisco, 1991).

6. Kenneth M. Ribin, ed., *Children's Play, New Directions for Child Development*, No. 9 (San Francisco: Jossey-Bass, 1980), pp. 17-23.

7. Catherine Garvey, *Play* (Cambridge, Mass.: Harvard University Press, 1977), pp. 17-23.

8. Arthur Koestler, *The Act of Creation* (New York: Macmillan Co., 1964).

9. Abraham Maslow, *The Farther Reaches of Human Nature* (New York: Viking Press, 1971).

10. Based on Proverbs 8:30-31.

11. Jean Piaget, *Play, Dreams and Imitation in Childhood* (New York: W. W. Norton, 1962). First Eng. ed., 1951.

12. Howard Gardner, *Art, Mind and Brain: A Cognitive Approach to Creativity* (New York: Basic Books, Inc. 1982), esp. ch. 4.

13. Taylor McConnell, "Cross-Cultural Ministries with Families," *Religious Education* 79:3 (Summer 1984): 358.

14. David L. Miller, *Gods and Games* (New York: Harper and Row, 1970).

15. Hugo Rahner, *Man at Play*, Eng. trans. (London: Barnes and Oates, 1965); original German, 1949.

16. An excellent introduction to the media history of the Bible is Thomas E. Boomershine, "Religious Education and Media Change: A Historical Sketch," *Religious Education* 82:2 (Spring 1987): 269-278.

17. A selection of books about the challenge of television to religion must include the following: Neil Postman, *Amusing Ourselves to Death: Public Discourse in the Age of Show Business* (New York: Viking Penguin, 1985); Gregor T. Goethals, *The TV Ritual: Worship at the Video Altar* (Boston: Beacon Press, 1981) and *The Electronic Golden Calf: Images, Religion, and the Making of Meaning* (Cambridge, Mass.: Cowley Publications, 1990); Hope Kelly and Howard Gardner, eds., *Viewing Children Through Television, New Directions for Child Development*, No. 13, William Damon, editor-in-chief (San Francisco: Jossey-Bass Inc., 1981); and the entire volume of *Religious Education* 82:2 (Spring 1987).

   An early but excellent overview of children and electronic media is Patricia Marks Greenfield, *Mind and Media: The Effects of Television, Computers and Video Games, The Developing Child*, Jerome Bruner, Michael Cole and Barbara Lloyd, eds. (Boston: Harvard University Press, 1984).

   Excellent resources, including important bibliographical materials, may be found by writing to the Center for Media and Values, 1962 South Shenandoah Street, Los Angeles, CA 70034.

18. Samuel Terrien, *The Elusive Presence: The Heart of Biblical Theology* (San Francisco: Harper and Row, 1978).

First Love
The Young Child's Prayer

by Patricia Coulter

Trying to companion little children along the path of prayer sometimes feels like traversing a tightrope; the child's way is often not our natural or preferred way.

[Editor's Note: The examples of children's prayers and remarks as well as the religious education methodology cited in this article are from the author's experience as a catechist in the Catechesis of the Good Shepherd program. In this method, the place of catechesis is called an atrium, reminiscent of the forecourt in early Christian basilicas where catechumens gathered before being admitted to the full eucharistic liturgy.]

The Spiritual Journey

"The Lord who gives us life established with us the baptismal covenant."[1]

Prayer is at the heart of the child's spiritual journey from the baptismal font to the eucharistic table. Prayer is like an inner stream that flows throughout this period of passage that the child makes during these most formative years of life, a period that involves an important transition time around the age of six.

Prayer, viewed in the larger framework of the child's spiritual journey, takes on a fuller light; it becomes more than a matter of "prayers" or "teaching children to pray." The young child's prayer, from the perspective of this underground stream, is seen in a new light. Other vital questions come into clearer relief: What is the source of the young child's prayer? Do little children have their own way of

---

Patricia Coulter is on the staff of the archdiocesan Office of Religious Education in Toronto. She is a lecturer and writer in the area of early childhood religious education.

praying? If so, what is it like? How do I companion little children along *their* path of prayer? How can I help the child's *own* way of praying?

If we center our reflections on the core dynamics in the child's prayer, we discover the operating principles on which to base our own practical applications in the sphere of home, school, or parish. Put another way: it is the dimension of the "who" and the "why" of young children's prayer that influences the "what to do" and "how to do it" concrete dimension of everyday life.

The Source Within

"The issue of prayer is not prayer; the issue of prayer is God"[2]: God, who is Love (cf. 1 Jn 4:8); the child, who is a "being-in-love"[3]; and their relationship together. It is a relationship in which it is God who loves "first" (cf. 1 Jn 4:19; Jn 15:16); God who takes the initiative: "We will come to him and make our dwelling with him" (Jn 14:23); and God who makes the overture of love to the child: "Because you are precious in my eyes and glorious, and because I love you" (Is 43:4). This is the context in which the young child's prayer lives and grows.

The Inner Wellspring

Perhaps, the first thing we can "do" to help the child's prayer is to "be" in a certain way. Parents and godparents, teachers and early childhood educators, pastors and pastoral teams, catechists and religious education directors—all of us who carry responsibility for the child's spiritual formation—are asked to trust that it does not depend on us alone.

The child has a personal *spiritual director*: " . . . the Spirit . . . will guide you" (Jn 16:13); an *inner teacher*: "[Y]ou are in me and I in you" (Jn 14:20); a *wellspring within*: " . . . the water I shall give will become in him a spring of water welling up . . . " (Jn 4:14); "Rivers of living water will flow from within . . . " (Jn 7:38). The young child, therefore, already *is* in relationship: "You have been my guide since I was first formed . . ." (Ps 22:10). It is a relationship that begins even before we see the child face-to-face: "Truly you have formed my inmost being; you knit me in my mother's womb" (Ps 139:13).

"The God of my gladness and joy" (Ps 43:4): How does the young child respond in this relationship? How does the young child receive the presence of God?

With *joy*: A six-year-old girl decides to make a collection of her own prayers, which she entitles: "Sara's Book of Joy."

With *wonder*: A group of young children are meditating on the parable of the woman and the leaven: "The kingdom of heaven is like yeast . . . " (Mt 13:33). After mixing two sets of dough—one with, the other without yeast—and leaving them for an hour, they come together to see what has happened to the yeast:

> "It changes every single way!" (Bradley)
> "It's [the dry yeast] so small!" (Monica)
> " . . . like a seed that becomes a tree! (Frankie)
> "It works!" (Ian)
> "One is sinking . . . one is rising fast!" (Andrew)

These "reactions" are more akin to "prayer responses."

With *insight*: Together with their teacher, a group of children is speaking about the symbols and gestures of baptism: light and water, the pouring of the water, and the signing of the cross. They begin to ponder the meaning of these "signs," such as the white baptismal garment that covers the child during the baptismal celebration. "Why is it so bright?" the teacher wonders aloud. Matthew Aaron, five years old, responds: "Because Jesus is light us . . . "

This way of pondering creates an atmosphere conducive to prayer since, "There is in the infant soul . . . a discernment of the unseen world in the things that are seen."[4]

With *deep enjoyment*: A young girl with multiple handicaps—physical and mental—takes out the wooden figures and sheepfold for the parable of the Good Shepherd. Gently, she moves the "sheep" in a gesture of following behind the "shepherd." As she does this, she speaks softly to herself: "He cares for Gary . . . he cares for John"; and then: "He leads Renee . . . he leads Gary . . . ," naming the children in her class. She continues like that for some time with an expression of quiet happiness on her face. Can this not be called "an experience of prayer"? "One who is loved generates love."[5]

These qualities that characterize the child's relationship with God are the hallmark of the young child's prayer as well. Therefore, the child's way of being in this relationship is also—inasmuch as prayer is response—the child's primary way of praying. Obvious though it may appear, the single most helpful aspect for us to know about the young child's prayer is that it is rooted in relationship. This is the heart of the child's prayer. As Karl Rahner writes so succinctly in his essay "What Does It Mean to Love Jesus":

> Yes, you see, you're actually only really dealing with Jesus when you throw your arms around him and realize right down to the bottom of your being that this is something you can still do today.[6]

This relationship is the mystery at the heart of the young child's prayer:

> I think one can and must love Jesus, in all immediacy and concretion, with a love that transcends space and time, in virtue of the nature of love in general and by the power of the Holy Spirit of God.[7]

This reality—the primacy of relationship and its primary "partners"—has many practical ramifications for us in helping the child's prayer. The first is that we are enabled to step off the tightrope onto solid earth! There is an element of mystery in all prayer; the child's is even more mysterious. How much of it does not "meet the eye"? How much of it remains unexpressed or unverbalized? Trying to companion little children along the path of prayer sometimes feels like traversing a tightrope; the child's way is often not our natural or preferred way.

There is an element of mystery in all prayer; the child's is even more mysterious. How much of it does not "meet the eye"? How much of it remains unexpressed or unverbalized?

It can be difficult for us to maintain our balance without leaning to one side ("I'm everything") or to the other side ("I m nothing"). To make the balancing act even more challenging: Has it ever seemed like you were weighed down with baggage that has accumulated gradually over your adult years, like a backpack getting heavier? And for those of us who are called to responsibility—in whatever way we are committed to companion the young child's prayer—it can seem as if we are burdened with an additional set of heavy luggage, too!

". . . [S]hine like lights in the world, as you hold onto the word of life . . ." (Phil 2:15-16). To see ourselves in this light and to let that light shine is what will help us get a secure footing on solid ground. When we recognize that prayer originates in the context of the God-child relationship, we realize that all that we do to nurture that relationship helps prayer; everything we do to help it unfold, feeds the child's inner wellsprings. Even more basic, by placing ourselves in the framework of that relationship, we open our own frontiers onto a space where it is first by being who we are that we support and contribute to the child's "prayer life": "The most marvelous of all things a being can do is to be."[8] This is true for the child and for us as well.

Companions on the Way

The second practical ramification occurs on the attitudinal level: looking at prayer in terms of the covenant between God and the child gives rise to an attitude of respect. Respect for the child's need for relationship, and thus for prayer, helps to create the climate where prayer truly flourishes. Respect for the child's capacities for prayer helps young children to pray in their own way.

Reflecting on this relationship also encourages an attitude of reverence. Reverence in itself communicates an eloquent message to the child. Even without words it says: You are in relationship. Someone is speaking to you personally. And reverence brings us a heightened awareness that the child's prayer is sacred ground.

Their Own Way

As we suggested, an important way to assist young children's prayer is to help them pray in their own way, to follow their own path in prayer. A desire to learn what this is, by our respectful looking, listening, and receiving, brings us unexpected gifts as well as helping the child. We are invited into a "childlike" prayer by the best possible "master": the little child.

If we were to sketch quickly a portrait, so to speak, of the young child's prayer, the following are some of the qualities that would emerge. The young child's prayer is essentially praise and thanksgiving. A five-year-old girl prays: "Dear Jesus, thank you for letting me be who I am because I love you and know you love me. Amen." The child's attention is centered, above all, on God's presence and acts of love; for the young child the "blessing" form of prayer predominates. A young boy proclaims: "You give your life to us"; and another young boy with him joins in: "You call us by our names."

In comparison with the prayer of praise, petitionary prayer is rare. "Asking" prayer does not seem to be the child's own prayer preference, and even when they are "asked" to pray, as in the following case, something of the true nature of the young child's prayer shines forth. This six-year-old boy was asked by his mother to pray for a co-worker's sick daughter. Later, the mother went to her son and asked: "Did you pray for the little girl who is sick?"

Son: "Yes."

Mother: "How did you pray for her?"

Son: "I said, 'O God, help the little girl who is sick.'"

Mother: "What's her name?"

Son: "I don't remember."

Mother: "How can you pray for her when you don't even remember her name?"

Son: "God knows her name, Mommy."

Usually, children pray with few words; oftentimes, the younger the child, the fewer the words. A young boy works intently with the paten and chalice (miniature representations of the vessels used in the liturgy of the Mass). At one point during this otherwise silent activity, he raises the chalice with great solemnity and says, "Father." He places it back on the table and sits silently with his eyes fixed on the chalice. Then, after a little while he says, "Amen." The words may be few, but they are rich in meaning.

A catechist shows the children the wooden figures representing the Good Shepherd parable. After spending time together with the children, reflecting on its message, she invites gently:

"How do we feel when we hear these words? . . . Is there anything we want to say to the Good Shepherd?" One child prays: "I love the Shepherd, and the Shepherd loves me"; another prays: "The Lord is my shepherd."

Young children have the capacity for extended prayer, the ability to rest in a recollected way for a prolonged period. A five-year-old child goes to the area of the atrium where the altar is located (less than child-sized replicas of the articles associated with the celebration of the eucharist). Carefully, he puts out all the objects: altar cloth, paten and chalice, candles, the cross of the risen Christ. After the candles are lighted, the child sits calmly looking at the light. He invites the catechist to be with him: "We should pray now." Then he suggests: "We should sing now. You sing with me." He begins a song of his own making, a gentle melody of praise. This homemade canticle continues for five stanzas, after which the catechist leaves. The child, however, remains there, slowly lifting the vessels—paten and chalice—in gestures of prayer. It continues for many minutes more like this in silence. From a distance, it could be seen that all of it—the gestures, the contemplative way of looking at the light, the posture of the body, the silence—was prayer for that young child; a child who had been diagnosed as "hyperactive" and considered by parents and teachers to be a "problem child."

Most of all, the child's prayer is joyful. Joy, sometimes muted, other times manifested clearly, is the undercurrent of the young child's prayer. In part, the delicacy of their joy is due to what G. K. Chesterton describes as the "two facts" about young children: "First, they are very serious, and secondly, that they are in consequence very happy."[9] The following is a simple example of this coexistence of happiness and seriousness.

It was the time of the Epiphany celebration. The children gathered together for a moment of prayer after meditating on the event of the coming of the Kings. One little girl mused happily: "And they brought beautiful gifts!" Reflectively, she searched for their names: "Jewels, gold, and . . . ," hesitating awhile, she murmured, "Frankin . . . stein." At this, the other young children whispered among themselves "Frankinstein?" without the predictable outburst of giggles. They seemed to sense her seriousness and waited as she tried to recall the word that had seemed so wonderful to her. "And frankincense," she proclaimed, smiling once again.

A Great Littleness

We know that prayer is a world filled with paradox. It is a world in which what is most valued in our "world" is turned upside down: taking charge and being in control are no longer assets, and poverty and vulnerability are no longer liabilities. Prayer is a world where who we "are" is more important than what we "do"; where productivity takes second place to relationship; surrender becomes more effective than effort. If this is true in our prayer, it is even more true in the prayer of young children.

The paradox we discover in their prayer is that greatness is hidden in littleness. That the young child has a huge hunger for love means a profound need to experience God's presence in prayer; that the young child has such a great capacity to enter into the covenant relationship means an ability to pray and enjoy prayer.

These needs and capacities of young children are our guide to helping their prayer. These can be summarized in two points. The first is a direct way of nourishing the child's prayer: helping the child to "read the signs" of the covenant relationship. The second is an indirect way of offering nurturance: learning ourselves how to "read the signs" of the child's relationship with God.

The first way requires our "direct" presence. This involves helping the child's direct access to the sources of God's own self-communication in the word (Scripture) and self-giving in the liturgy (signs and symbols, gestures and objects). Some of the biblical "signs" we help the child to read are found in the parables. The parable of the Good Shepherd (see Jn 10) describes the "face" of God the child most seeks and offers the aspect of God's love the child most needs—a protective reassuring Presence, a relationship of unlimited and personal love (the elements of the "wolf" and "hired hand" are introduced to children generally after the age of six).

The parable of the "found" sheep (see Lk 15:4-7) reveals a particular dimension of the Good Shepherd's infinite love (he knows if even "one sheep" is missing and cannot rest until he has searched for and found it). This Good News is received as yet another proof of the Good Shepherd's personal and protective love for the child (only *after* six years of age does the child enter into the "moral element" of this parable—how or why the sheep gets lost—and, therefore, the young child's attention is not and should not be drawn to this "moral" aspect).

The parables of the mustard seed and the leaven (see Mt 13:31-33) reveal the mystery and marvel of how the kingdom grows; the parables of the "precious pearl" and hidden treasure (see Mt 13:44-46) reveal the beauty of its inestimable value. Other biblical "signs" of the covenant relationship are the accounts of the events surrounding the announcement and birth of Jesus and the prophecies that heralded these events (see Is 9:1); the greatest event, the resurrection of Christ, especially Luke's account of the "empty tomb" (see Lk 24:1-12); verses from the psalms that are rich in symbolism, especially Psalm 23 and Psalm 27:1.

Another direct way to nourish the child's prayer is to help the child discover and experience the interconnectedness of these biblical signs in everyday living, in "ordinary" time. There are some simple ways to do this. Provide or prepare simple materials that the child can "use" (i.e., have direct contact with wood, cloth, or paper; images/pictures of "light"; a statue or replica of a "shepherd," a "pearl," and so forth). The activity with these materials becomes a way into prayer.

Reverence in itself communicates
an eloquent message to the child.
Even without words, it says:
You are in relationship.

Sometimes, the "doing" is prayer itself, especially in the case of the liturgical elements. Take the child to church (outside the time of communal worship) for a personal guided tour; point out the paschal candle, the symbol of the resurrection of Christ (the "Liturgy of Light," which begins the Easter Vigil celebration, can be adapted easily and effectively for young children). Relate this to the child's own baptismal candle, a symbol of the time when the light/life of the risen Christ "came to me." Also identify the objects associated with the eucharist and baptism.[10] Each year, remember the anniversary of the child's baptism with a short ritual involving the lighting of the child's baptismal candle. This can become an important annual celebration for the child, godparents, and family members.

Compile a photo album of the child's baptism, with pictures of the different moments in the rite and the persons who shared in its celebration, and tell the "true story" of that significant event in the child's own "salvation history."

The second way to nurture the child's prayer invites our "indirect" presence by enabling the child to have his or her own personal prayer experience. We can help by preparing a place and objects for prayer and by providing personal "space" and silence. It does not take much room or many "things," just the "bare necessities": some small place (even just a shelf) in the home for a

Bible, a candle, a flower, an image (e.g., of the risen Christ or an icon of the Madonna and Child); some small space or place in the child's own room where things—preferably of the child's own choosing—are easily seen and readily accessible. Allow the child time and space to use the materials and activities that help "concretize" the Good News.

Once again, it requires only the most "essential" of things. In the classroom, for example, have a small area for seasonal articles such as the Advent wreath, the paschal candle, and the Nativity set; a prayer table with a colored cloth and flowers to match the liturgical season (white for Christmas, red for Pentecost, etc.); and other simple things that the children may use themselves such as the Nativity set with a packet of drawings to trace or color, a small book to look at, a prayer card with a word or line from Scripture ("Hosanna," "Gloria"), and so on. Be ready and willing to step aside so as to allow the inner dialogue between God and the child to unfold, especially if some of the above-mentioned aspects are present (which provide an "atmosphere" for prayer).

Create a prayerful climate for the child by setting aside a time in the day—both at home and at school—where "silence" is provided and encouraged. This means providing the "absence" of noise (e.g., radio or TV) and encouraging the "presence" of prayer (e.g., soft music to "introduce" the time set aside for prayer; a cushion, rug, or prayer corner; lighting a candle, dimming the lights).

Reading the "signs" is the key that unlocks the door to prayer for the young child: to know that everything in the Bible and the liturgy (all the images and objects and gestures) contains a personal message for me from Someone for whom I am everything. This is food and drink for the child's prayer journey.

The Door

"To pray is to open a door where both God and the soul may enter" (A. J. Heschel). There is also a key that helps us to open the door for the child's prayer. The key for us is to realize that the child is already on the journey and comes well equipped with all the necessary tools. For example, powerful inner directives impel the child's interest toward language. Biblical and liturgical words, therefore, have great impact on the child. Introducing "prayers" in the context of their biblical source is helpful for the child. An example would be saying the "Our Father" phrase by phrase, with intervals that vary according to the child's need and desire to "hear more." We can begin with "Our Father who art in heaven"; then add, "Hallowed be the name," and so on, telling the child when and why Jesus taught this prayer (see Lk 11:1-4) and helping the child to "taste" (cf. Ps 34:9) the richness of the words a few at a time.

Young children have strong sensitivities that propel and focus their attention on movement. Liturgical and other prayer gestures hold immense interest for the child. Some other examples, as well as those already referred to are the following: the signing of the cross on the forehead, lips, and heart before hearing the gospel; the "kissing" of the Bible (at Mass, the priest honors the Lectionary with this gesture); the invocation of the Holy Spirit (the out-stretched hands over the bread and wine at Mass, over the water during the baptismal rite). The child is predominantly a sensorial being who absorbs and explores everything relating to touch, sight, sound, taste, and smell; touching and "doing" the smell of incense and beeswax, the candle's flame, the sound of bells and music are all entrance ways to, and avenues for, prayer.

The child is rooted and grows best in accordance with an inner need for order. Therefore, the rhythm of routine in prayer and a ritual of regular times for prayer are delightful for children.

These are the powerful dynamics operative in the child's prayer. In the measure that we support and work with them, to that degree, then, our presence is fruitful and effective in helping the child's prayer. Our confidence, however, comes from the fact that prayer primarily depends on the secret spring within the young child:

> Because there is in the child,
> there is in childhood a unique grace,
> An entirety, a firstness
> That is total,
> An origin, a secret, a spring, a point of departure,
> A beginning which might be called absolute.
> Children are new creatures.[11]

It is a spring whose source is a Person—the Holy Spirit (cf. Rm 8:16)—and which flows unfailingly in us as well, even when "we do not know how to pray . . ." (Rm 8:26).

Suggested Reading

Cavalletti, Sofia. *The Religious Potential of the Young Child.* Patricia M. and Julie M. Coulter, trans.; preface by Mark Searle. Chicago: Liturgy Training Publications, 1992.

The Holy Bible (particularly, the books of the gospels and the book of psalms). As well as "reading" (which, as a wise spiritual director indicated, can sometimes be like "looking at a cookbook: it is tantalizing but doesn't do much to feed our hunger . . . "), choose whatever translation most helps you to "pray" the Sacred Scriptures.

The *Order of Mass.* Read the actions and prayers of the eucharistic liturgy in the manner suggested above.

The Rite of Baptism: For One Child and for Several Children. Collegeville, Minn.: The Liturgical Press, 1970. A helpful way to read a liturgical text—if such an analogy will be permitted—is like watching a video of a baptismal celebration, once with the sound off, and a second time without the "picture" but with the sound on. For instance, read through the baptismal rite, looking only at the symbols and gestures involved; at another time, listen attentively to the prayers of the celebration. This is also a helpful way to approach liturgy with young children. The (silent) symbols and gestures speak volumes—because this is the language that has most immediate impact; the words of prayer accompanying these are then heightened in their meaning as well.

Notes

1. St. Basil the Great, *On the Holy Spirit,* ch. 15 and 35. See *The Divine Office: The Liturgy of the Hours II,* Lent and Eastertide (Dublin: Talbot Press), p. 557.

2. Abraham Heschel, *Man's Quest for God* (New York: Scribner's, 1954), p. 58.

3. Cf. Josef Pieper, *About Love,* Richard and Clara Winston, trans. (Chicago: Franciscan Herald Press, 1972). In referring to the biblical passage we have just cited (1 Jn 4:19), Pieper poses an important question about the one who is loved by God (in our case, the young child). "In love *with whom,* we are inclined to ask; or should it be: in the love *of whom?* . . . the trait of 'being-in-love' exists and fundamentally affects man's relationship to the

universe" (p. 13). Further on, he writes, "It is God, who in the act of creation anticipates all conceivable human love and said: 'I will you to be; it is good, very good (Gn 1:31) that you exist.' He has already infused everything that human beings can love and affirm, goodness along with existence, and that means lovability and affirmability" (p. 25).

4. John Henry Cardinal Newman, "The Mind of Little Children" in *Miscellanies: From the Oxford Sermons and Other Writings* (Edinburgh: John Grant, 1898), p. 207.

5. From the "Discourse on the Holy Theophany," Nn. 2,6-8, attributed to St. Hippolytus. *Divine Office*, Vol. I, p. 338.

6. Karl Rahner, SJ, "What Does It Mean to Love Jesus?" *In the Love of Jesus and the Love of Neighbor*, Robert Barr, trans. (New York: Crossroad Publishing Company, 1983), p. 23. Rahner includes a line here that could be described as the chief characteristic of the young child's disposition in prayer: ". . . Jesus himself, the concrete person . . . can come right up close to us as the concrete, historical person he is—on the condition that we *want* to love him, that we have the courage to throw our arms around him."

7. Ibid., p. 23.

8. Etienne Gilson, *History of Christian Philosophy* (London: 1955), p. 83. Josef Pieper remarks that first and foremost, it is our attitude that matters. In this context, our "love need not necessarily be 'materialized' in specific acts of beneficence. What is at any rate *more decisive* [emphasis mine] is that concern and approval that are given from the very core of existence—we need not hesitate to say, which come from the heart—and which are directed toward the core of existence, the heart, of the child" (op. cit., pp. 27-28).

9. Gilbert Keith Chesterton, "A Defence of Baby-Worship" in *The Defendant* (London: J. M. Dent & Sons, Ltd., n.d.), p. 149. Another insight that follows directly after this is: "The gravity of the very young child . . . is the gravity of astonishment at the universe."

10. Sofia Cavalletti, *The Religious Potential of the Young Child: To Six*, Patricia M. and Julie M. Coulter, trans.; preface by Mark Searle (Chicago: Liturgy Training Publications, 1992). Chapter 7 is dedicated to the young child's prayer.

11. Charles Peguy, "Innocence and Experience" in *Basic Verities: Prose and Poetry*, Ann and Julien Green, trans. (New York: Books for Libraries Press, 1972), p. 227.

With New Song and Festive Dance: Celebration and Ritual in the Home

by Joan Halmo

> The home has the unique ability to open the personal and familial dimensions of life to explicitly religious aspects.

Festivity and Ritual

The child walks with wonder among the ordinary things of life, pausing to delight in the things that adults often take for granted, stopping to discover and rejoice. Filled with fantasy and imagination, capable of continual and sustained amazement, the young child is at ease in the timeless world of festivity.[1] Among children, there can be true festivity in every day, and in the moments within each day.

Appreciating and celebrating the moment as gift is a capability not highly prized in our day and in our society, for we are often part of a very complex lifestyle and absorbed by the world of daily care. For some, celebration could even be construed as a waste of time. It disrupts the ordinary routine and produces nothing of significance in terms of accomplishment. As the philosopher Josef Pieper writes, however, the rational, useful world that so holds our attention is but a partial environment for our humanity. Our human fulfillment lies in transcending the purely pragmatic, the visible and verifiable, in order to embrace the whole as marvelous gift.[2] Encountering that gift, the mystery of life, we can leave behind temporarily the workaday world of labor and practicality and enter into the apparent uselessness of festivity, laughter, extravagance, absence of calculation. Historically, this free and freeing space without boundaries came to be called "holy day"—

Joan Halmo, liturgist, musician, and author, resides in Saskatoon, Saskatchewan, Canada.

now, holiday. The true holiday is a time that partakes of sacred timelessness and nourishes humanity through companionship with the Divine, making us whole.

At the same time as unbounded horizons of celebration beckon to us, there is another need that manifests itself: the yearning for the familiar, for structure and order and the repetition of what is known. There is a "human need to concur on a set of symbols and rituals that create order, give identity, and provide motivation."[3] We assemble complexes of gestures and words and invest them with meaning. We call them *ritual*. Repeated and perpetuated, they become our tradition. They serve to mark occasions large and small in our lives, from the passing of days and nights, from hellos and good-byes, to births and birthdays and anniversaries, to goals achieved and life journeys ended. Making ritual is a creative act. It is fundamental in human life, and it emerges as a phenomenon in both the life of individuals and the social group.

Young children engage constantly in ritual, and they create their own or oblige others to help them do so. We can witness this on the most ordinary level. "Again, again, the same way," they say; or, "I always keep it on this shelf"; or, to the adult blithely reading aloud a familiar tale, "You missed a word in the story!" Rather than being bored by what is predictable, children relish it, finding there a sense of personal security and pleasure in the recurrence of something that seems ever as fascinating as if it had not happened before. Repetition and familiarity, then, are an important need in the life of children. Indeed, the discovery and creation of order are necessities for all human life and a reflection of the first divine word in the book of Genesis, where God makes order of darkness and chaos (cf. Gn 1-2).

The Unique Contribution of the Home

In the home, events of family and daily life as well as the events of the greater Christian family—the Church—and its liturgical time can be the occasion for celebration and prayer. From the household's daily routines of rising, eating, working, playing, and sleeping, to the Church's great days and seasons, the household can take part in ritual that enriches and strengthens the individual and the family. The home has the unique ability to open the personal and familial dimensions of life to explicitly religious aspects. A Christian family not only marks birthdays and assorted anniversaries in a secular way, but blesses God for the gift of life and for every passing year of grace. The Christian home provides the step that goes beyond gratitude and wonder in a general sense to the praise and thanks of God. One moves from the gift to the giver; one transcends the object by looking to and worshiping its Source.[4] Spontaneous prayer or prayer forms derived from our tradition—biblical and liturgical—can articulate the Christian meaning of the event. Several fine books containing suggestions for prayer and ceremony on special family and personal occasions are available.[5]

Of all the domestic rituals that form us as family and teach us about community, none is as powerful as the meal.

It is within the rhythm of daily living and within family relationships that we learn many of the gestures and rituals that are integral to the public worship we call liturgy. We come to know what it means to gather as community, to welcome, to forgive and be forgiven, to rejoice or mourn together, to thank, to assemble around a table to be nourished, to promise one another care and service. The sensitivity and purposeful intent with which these actions are carried out in the home are the foundation for the child's assimilation of attitudes essential to the Christian assembly at worship.

Of all the domestic rituals that form us as family and teach us about community, none is as powerful as the meal. Day by day, the table is where we gather not only to nurture our physical life but also to reach out to one another, tell our day's stories, remember the past or look ahead; we share food for our physical selves and also the food of community, human communing. The domestic table is the basic sacrament for the child and for the household. At the family table, we learn gradually what is done at the eucharistic table of the larger family, the Church. In all this, the value and beauty of common symbols emerge; in the meal shared, the family treasures simple gifts: food and drink and one another's presence.

Another important ritual in family as well as in the church community is that of family storytelling. An affirmation and celebration of roots, the telling of the family story at home happens in many ways.

Parents can recount the major milestones of the family's life, perhaps supplementing these with photos and mementos. On occasions like birthdays, the family highlights the honored person's individual journey of life. In between formal moments of story sharing, there are the spontaneous "Remember when . . . " moments, offering even the little ones the opportunity to contribute their familial reminiscences. Young children love the repeated telling of favorite tales, about themselves particularly but about family and relatives as well. The young child is more attuned than many an adult to the oral preliterate tradition (on which the Scriptures themselves are founded) and is one of the best listeners to a well-told story!

In highlighting the importance of table and word, we touch on two fundamental dimensions that are at the heart of most human celebrations. It is not surprising that the eucharist itself from very early times has been comprised of these elements,[6] and that Vatican Council II spoke of the liturgy of the word and the liturgy of the table.[7] The way we foster these aspects of table and word day by day shapes how our children are capable of entering into liturgical life. As Gabe Huck writes, "We are able to find holiness in the bread that is blessed and shared in the assembly of Christians only if we find holiness in all the fruit of the earth by which we are nourished and brought together.[8] Likewise, by becoming listeners in the entire scope of our lives, we prepare ourselves to come with openness to God's word proclaimed in the assembly.

Liturgy as Resource for Celebration in the Home

The liturgical life of the Church, with its rituals and symbols, its Scripture and prayer and song, is an inexhaustible source of spirituality and of imagery both for young children and their families. Using the liturgy of the Church as a primary resource for home celebration has great benefits. The liturgy provides a language of prayer and praise. It is a language associated with generations of Christians before us, allowing us in a way to walk beside them, the host of God's saints. Liturgically oriented prayer and celebration in the household integrate the life of the home with that of the parish, so that home and church are closely linked and mutually reinforced in the child's experience. Lastly and above all, as we keep annually the feasts and seasons with all their theological and spiritual richness, liturgy gradually forms us as Christian persons and as a Christian people.

Liturgical texts—the scriptural readings, the psalms of the feast or season, or prayers (for instance, the opening prayer used at a given eucharist)—can provide both words and the images from which family celebration might draw inspiration. Selection of a very limited number of these is sufficient for use with young children for whom repetition of text and music is extremely important. A whole season may be summarized for the household in the use of one particular song or prayer as table blessing: for the Fifty Days of Easter, the psalm verse, "This is the day that the Lord has made: let us be glad and rejoice in it!" (responsorial psalm refrain, First Sunday of Easter); for all of Lent, "We do not live on bread alone, but on every word that comes from the mouth of God" (gospel acclamation, First Sunday of Lent). A personal or household anniversary can be summed up and given a motif, also using liturgical/biblical texts: "Give thanks to the Lord for he is good, for his mercy endures forever!" (responsorial psalm refrain, Second Sunday of Easter).

Activities connected to the feast or season are a way of extending the liturgical celebration into the daily context of the home and into the energetic life of the young child. Domestic resources and family activities—music and dance, arts and crafts, the enjoyment of nature, the preparation and sharing of food—all these can unabashedly be part of celebrating faith and can help the little child experience the joyous breadth of Christian living. Thus, the family can shape its common prayer, its activities, and even occasionally its mealtime menu on the predominant ideas of a liturgical feast or season. Sunday, for instance, can be welcomed with a ceremonial reading of the gospel on Saturday evening; Easter at home can include a glorious paschal candle decorated by the child; Lent can be made more memorable in the crossed-arm pretzels that symbolize the call to prayer; Christmas can be a time of appreciating nature's light and all lights as reminders of Jesus, promised Light of the World; and Advent's days of waiting can actually be seen and counted in the progressive lighting of the four candles on the Advent wreath.

While deepening its understanding of the spirit of a feast or season, each family can create its own pattern of rituals and customs incorporating the interests, the customs, and perhaps the ethnic background of that family.

To help in this enterprise of establishing some distinctive family ways of marking the liturgical times, parents can gradually assemble for their own resources a few select books, the guideline for their purchase being quality rather than quantity. The home should have a Bible in a translation easily understandable to children—actually, the translation used in parish liturgy is best for home as well, as it gives the child the opportunity to become familiar with the same phrasing of the scriptural word.

Also important to have are a list of the readings for Sundays and feasts of the church year (these are sometimes given in the back of liturgically oriented family prayer books) and some type of resource that provides suggestions for the Liturgy of the Hours, especially morning and evening prayer, along with texts and songs for various occasions. A small well-chosen hymnal that contains at least a good number of the selections used in the parish is a long-term spiritual asset in the home.[9]

> Using the liturgy of the Church as
> a primary resource for home celebration
> has great benefits. The liturgy provides
> a language of prayer and praise.

Useful too for the household is a book that suggests ways of expanding on liturgical ideas and imagery through arts, crafts, games, group events, and so on. The latter type of book needs to be rooted strongly in the best liturgical tradition. One judges the soundness of such a volume largely by where its main emphases lie and by the propriety of its suggestions. Is there a disproportionate amount of space given to Advent and nothing to the Sunday or the paschal triduum, both of which are far older and more important in our tradition? Do the symbols suggested for home use correspond to the times at which they appear in the parish liturgy—for instance, the Christmas tree for Christmas-Epiphany time and not during Advent, the paschal candle for the third day of triduum and the Easter season and not on Ash Wednesday? Books of excellent sacred art—mosaics, medieval illuminations, stained glass, and paintings of the masters—intrigue children and can often be procured for the home from sale tables or used book shops. A parent can always be alert also for children's books that explore aspects of Christian spirituality or that present biblical and other stories of our faith tradition in an exceptionally fine way.[10]

Cassette tapes and records of music suitable for all kinds of occasions within the family can be either purchased or borrowed from the local library. It is good to expose young children to a wide range of sacred music, the earlier styles as well as contemporary, Gregorian chant to J. S. Bach to Christopher Walker, and everyone in between. This is, of course, a contribution to the child's aesthetic development. Beyond that, from a religious viewpoint, a broadly inclusive approach offers the child and the family a glimpse of the profound beauty and spiritual insight in the sacred music of God's people across the ages.

Some simple home decor and supplies that can be collected over time and kept from year to year are also an asset. A parent might invest gradually in objects such as an icon or another piece of fine religious art for the child's room; an Advent wreath form; or a festal tablecloth of dazzling colors, which could be the Sunday/Easter linen. For arts and crafts to be made, there need to be the usual paper and glue supplies. In addition, a parent might save from year to year the better and sturdier things that the children themselves have made: drawings and cards and other art pieces (these can be laminated for greater permanence) or decorations for the Christmas tree or Easter baskets. One can make something of a hobby of collecting, adapting, and creating items as well as ideas for the celebrative purposes of one's family!

Beginning Ritual and Common Prayer in the Home

From the very beginning of a family's life together, time-honored prayers and gestures from our tradition can be used. One of these prayers, stemming from biblical roots, is the parental blessing of the child. The parent could place a hand on the child's head or, if desired, trace the cross on the child's forehead, saying a simple blessing such as: "May God bless you, N_____"; or one with more extended wording such as that from Numbers 6:24-26:

The LORD bless you and keep you!
The LORD let his face shine upon you, and be gracious to you!
The LORD look upon you kindly and give you peace!

This could be both a good-night blessing for children and a good-bye wish prayed when waving farewell to friends or relatives departing the home.

Table prayers are, of course, an excellent time for children to begin participating in community prayer. A spoken table grace or a seasonal song may serve as both a moment of remembering God, the fountain of all good things, and as an occasion of family communion in prayer. Song at meals is a natural place to introduce family singing for households, for everyone is usually present and common prayer here is an accepted practice.

The role of song in religious experience is very significant. Recalling their childhood faith formation at an international meeting recently, a study group of eighteen adults found very little in common in their early spiritual development, except that for each of them, religious music made a distinct impact, which they remembered after many years. To sing is to add an important dimension to the child's lived experience of faith. To sing is to increase the vividness and memorability of the prayer text. In an age when community song is so rare in both domestic and social life, to sing at the family table might be virtually the sole training ground for the Church's expression in song. Perhaps the home will find itself responsible for maintaining the tradition of song needed to revitalize and foster parish singing! If possible, it is desirable to use the same liturgical antiphons, psalms, and songs as sung in one's parish to unify and strengthen the child's experience of the Church's feasts and seasons.

If a household finds that it can pray communally on a regular basis, family members could assemble in the morning or after the evening meal for a short prayer time. The prayer could be modelled on the structure of the Liturgy of the Hours, the Church's official prayer. An abbreviated form designed for the presence and participation of young children follows.

Call to Prayer

Leader: Come, let us worship the Lord!

All: Let us praise his goodness and love!

Psalm: For example, Psalm 23, "The Lord is my shepherd." (One verse is sufficient if children are very young.)

Scripture: Choose a gospel passage, perhaps selected verses

Reading: From the previous Sunday's gospel. (Or, if the prayer is part of a Sunday welcoming service held on Saturday evening, the gospel of the following day is anticipated.)

Canticle: For morning, Zechariah's Canticle (Lk 2:68-79); for evening, Mary's Canticle (Lk 2:46-55)

Intercessions: Keep them short, and invite everyone to present people and their needs before God.

Blessing: [Given by a parent in these or similar words]

      The Lord bless us and keep us all in his love.

All: Amen.

The more formal prayers suggested above need, of course, to be part of an atmosphere of prayer in the home, part of an ease in speaking of and to the Lord. Such informal prayer or spiritual conversation frequently arises from everyday experiences. Is it a beautiful morning? We are grateful to God for this gift and all the marvelous things that are around us. Something sad befalls us? We accept it as best we can, embrace one another, knowing that God is near. Someone is ill or dies? We know the Lord, the Good Shepherd, cares for that person and for each of us in our need.

Keeping the Liturgical Cycle,
with Sunday as Starting Point

The celebration of the liturgical cycle in the home can be a rich source of spiritual insight for both the child and the family. The sacred rhythms of the week and the year can be an admirable way of initiating the child into the enjoyment of belonging to the Lord. In choosing which festive times to keep, we need not proceed chronologically through the church year. Instead, there is a hierarchy that is evident in the order of evolution of the Church's major feasts and seasons, for the historical order of development reveals theological priorities.[11] First, there is the paschal mystery, the Lord's passing through suffering and death to the glory of resurrection, and each Christian's sharing in this *pasch* through sacrament and a life lived by the gospel. This central event of the paschal mystery is celebrated weekly on Sunday, and annually in the paschal cycle, comprised of the paschal triduum, the Fifty Days of Easter, and the preparation time called Lent. Next, there is the Christmas cycle: the Christmas-Epiphany feasts and season, and their preparation time, Advent. If parents have only a limited amount of energy for liturgical endeavors with their children, they might best use it in celebrating the Sunday worthily, all year long. If parents have another portion of strength to expend, the paschal triduum would be next, and so on, down the liturgical line (the preparation periods for a given season are of less importance than the season itself, so that the greater emphasis should be, for instance, on keeping Christmas-Epiphany than on Advent alone).

The present discussion will focus only on the Sunday. The principles by which the spirit of Sunday can infuse and shape the day can be used by readers as a model for home celebrations of other feasts and seasons. One tries to discover the origins and essential meaning of a given feast and to acquire an understanding of the images and spirit that can be shaped into the family celebration.

For the Christian Church, the primary and original feast day is Sunday. It is the day of the resurrection, on which the Lord rose and on which his followers thereafter have gathered for the eucharist. Thus, essentially, the Lord's Day and the Lord's supper belong together. Sunday is first and foremost for the eucharist. Like the disciples of the Lord on the way to Emmaus, the community recognizes its risen Lord in the breaking of the bread (cf. Lk 24:13-35). Sometimes known as "the eighth day" because it breaks beyond our usual calendar cycles of time, Sunday is full of the presence of the risen Christ and gives us a taste of eternity in his presence. It is the day of God's creation of light, and of the true Light and new creation who is Christ. It is the day the Lord has made and we rejoice in it (cf. Ps 118:24). In sum, every Sunday is Easter and Easter is every Sunday. The Sunday was held in such regard by our ancestors in faith that they could exclaim: "We cannot live without the Sunday!"[12] What, then, are the images and key ideas surrounding the Sunday? Easter, *pasch* or passover, resurrection, eucharist, light, creation, eternity, and "alleluia" forever.[13]

To sing is to increase the vividness and memorability of the prayer text.

The awareness of Sunday as a day different from the others in the week could begin in the prayer made with the child at night-time or morning, when the adult could draw attention to the unique meaning of the day. The Church's long-standing manner of greeting the Sunday (and other great feasts as well) is with the prayer of the Liturgy of the Hours on Saturday evening, much as the Jewish people have welcomed the Sabbath with ceremony on the preceding evening. The Christian "First Vespers of Sunday" (so named to distinguish it from the Vespers—evening prayer—of Sunday proper) is the Church's common evening prayer, pointing forward to and already sharing in the Lord's Day. Immediately after supper on Saturday, the family could gather for a brief Vesper service, whose links with Sunday and the "Easter-ness" of Sunday are the lighting of the household paschal candle at the beginning of the service; the singing of a psalm, such as Psalm 122, "I rejoiced because they said to me, 'We will go up to the house of the Lord'"; and the proclamation of all or a portion of the Sunday gospel (for the evening prayer, the form suggested above could be used).

It is also possible to use the Jewish Sabbath ritual as an inspiration for a Sunday-welcoming meal to be held on Saturday evening. The lighting of the household paschal candle at the family table and the gospel reading could be complemented with the sharing of bread and a cup of wine or juice—the ties with Sunday eucharist are very apparent. Two or three families could gather occasionally for a common celebration of this meal.

The family can prepare together in a number of ways for Sunday's central moment, the eucharistic liturgy. These ways could include finding and filling a Sunday envelope for the monetary collection (older children who receive an allowance might regularly add some money of their own) or selecting food from the family's own supply cupboard for the Church's sharing box. Contributing both money and food for the support of the church community and the poor are part of the venerable Christian tradition, and taking the gifts to the church and presenting them in the eucharistic assembly are an important formative action for the child. The home's preparation for the Sunday could include even such personal necessities as the Saturday night bath and the setting out of Sunday clothes—best clothes, however simple they may be—or merely having a young child shine all the shoes for Sunday.

Choosing a time for Sunday eucharist that allows for the family's most focused and lively participation is important. Many parents with young children find that the best time to celebrate eucharist with their parish is the mid-morning. The children are fresh and rested, and there can be less sense of haste when the day arranges itself around the liturgical celebration. On the way to the Sunday liturgy, the family could sing an "alleluia" or an Easter song, the latter being always "in season" on a Sunday. Perhaps, the family might speak together of gathering around Jesus the Shepherd, who calls us and feeds us with his word and with the bread and cup, which are his very life. The eucharistic celebration itself can be presented in more detail at home to the very young child in terms of the Good Shepherd, as Sofia Cavalletti explains in *The Religious Potential of the Child*.[14] Finally, on the Sunday, it is ideal to arrive early enough at the church building to take time to walk around there, to visit the various centers for liturgical action, to meet some of the other members of the assembly, or simply to foster the child's familiarity with the "house of the Church," as it was called in ancient times.

Extending the message of the Sunday word at home can take different forms. If the child has heard the gospel reading of the day at a Sunday-welcoming service at home, he or she might easily remember a passage of the reading proclaimed at liturgy and share it with the family. Perhaps, the parent could sing with the child the refrain of the Sunday responsorial psalm; this could be done on the way home from Sunday eucharist and also during the week. This is an excellent way to provide the child with some of the phrases of biblical prayer and to use the Sunday psalm in the manner described so beautifully in the late fourth century by John Chrysostom: The psalm refrain becomes like a walking stick, which we carry along home and which can support us spiritually during the whole week.[15] Older preschoolers are usually able to remember something from the homily of the day (it is hoped that the latter has included some thoughts comprehensible even to the child). A striking line from the gospel of the day or the psalm refrain or an idea gleaned from the homily could be printed on a large paper and mounted on the refrigerator or in another place in the home where everyone will see it frequently throughout the week.

Sometimes, if the Sunday gospel has been especially vivid in its imagery, if the family is in a mood of reflective quiet, and if the child is not overly weary, a parent could spend some gospel-telling time with the child, either on the Sunday or later in the week. The Sunday gospel story could be told and discussed, then expressed in a drawing or in a symbol (often, a child prefers to express its spiritual understanding in a nonverbal manner). For suggestions in finding symbols related to the Sunday gospels, Gaynell Cronin's *Sunday throughout the Week* is helpful.[16]

Family mealtimes on Sunday can be made more special to underline the Easter character of the day. The paschal candle could be lit at all Sunday meals, and the table prayer could be a sung "alleluia" or a resurrection-oriented prayer. As often as is feasible, one can try to serve something in a festal way at each meal. A household might establish its own customs of Sunday foods centering on family favorites.[17] Sunday supper can be made as elaborate as the family's day allows, using the best table linens and dishes. From time to time, children could be invited to make decorated placecards, a centerpiece, or a more elaborate dessert for the family.

Sunday in its Christian origins was not primarily a day of rest but, rather, a day of eucharistic worship. In our time, with so many societal factors eroding the family's time together for leisure, prayer, and other activities in common, it is most fitting that the Sunday be seen as a day set apart for rejuvenation and refreshment in the Lord and in the community. Making a clear option for the special observance of Sunday as a holy day in the home can sometimes be difficult and is certainly not an obvious route to take in our society. As Bishop Joseph Fiorenza writes, "For many, [making this option] will require a new and fresh way of thinking and acting. . . . Sunday has a sacred character which must not be eclipsed by commercial or profane interests."[18] Family members could spend time more liberally with one another, with friends or relatives. There should be time to visit the sick, call on an aged friend, phone someone in need, invite a lonely person to share a meal, or just be in touch again with old friends. There should be space to enjoy music, the arts, sports, and recreation. At least on occasion, this is a day to take off watches and ignore the clock, abandon agendas, and taste the freedom of the timeless eternity of which Sunday is a sign!

Conclusion

The home that provides a matrix for celebration and ritual has to be expressive of Christian values in other aspects of living, lest children learn the falsehood that religion and life are separable from one another. We need to strive communally toward prevention of the kind of impression offered to Robert Coles by a young boy: "you can be religious and bad. . . ."[19] A family's examination of its life-style choices will benefit much from a book such as *Parenting for Peace and Justice* by Kathleen and James McGinnis.[20] The following are some initial questions to pose in the family's ongoing search to let gospel values transform its lifestyle:

- Are we freeing ourselves from inordinate preoccupation with possessions in order to nurture inner resources, spiritual receptivity, and personal relationships?

- Are we working toward greater simplicity in the family's food and clothing usage and encouraging a generally appreciative attitude in each person?

- Among our children, do we foster creativity and new skills rather than rely on passive entertainment and expensive toys?

- What games and toys do we present to our children— those based on violence and war or those that teach attitudes of cooperation and peace?

- Are we nurturing the child's pleasure in nature into an attitude of environmental responsibility?

- In our family relationships, is there an effort to emphasize positive behavior, to affirm consciously, to express affection, to listen and to share, to resolve conflict in nonviolent ways?

☐ How are we handling the ongoing task of accepting a wide range of differences in people: race, gender, age, various physical and mental abilities?

☐ Do we involve young children in direct service to persons at hand—feeding the hungry, visiting the sick, and so on—thus, awakening an awareness of broader social responsibility?

In sum, it is impossible to pray for peace and sing of salvation if all of us, young and old, are not about the business of establishing in some way the reign of peace, justice, and truth.

How can one ever hope for time to do all this, to take time to wonder and celebrate and in the same breath to carry on the work of building the kingdom? Not all parents will have the same amount of time to spend with their children; not all parents will have the luxury of choosing whether or not to work outside the home. However, in the time that is available, something can be done. Choices will have to be made for a particular lifestyle, one that leaves time for the things that are important for a family that cherishes and intends to foster Christian values. Special times for activities or sharing will have to be protected vigorously against inroads from daily tasks and unnecessary interruptions. A parent must be flexible enough, nevertheless, to respond to the needs of a child who may be tired or totally engaged in another type of activity at the very time the adult designates for a shared spiritual time. As always with children, schedules and people need to be malleable, and the best-laid plans should be adjusted with sensitivity and patience! Probably one of the hardest things to opt for firmly and to carry out regularly is the family meal (although it is easier when children are very young to achieve the goal of at least one family meal daily than it is when children are older and involved in more activities outside the home). Instinctively, we know that when something critical is at stake, if there is a will, there is almost always a way. In the end, it is often a question of decision, decisiveness, and the commitment and the courage to assume what is really a counter-cultural stance.

Because of the pluralism in today's society, many families engaged in the Christian journey seek the support of other families with children of similar age. It is desirable that children have peers for whom a Christian frame of reference and Christian values are operative. It is ideal to know others for whom the rhythms of life and of the ecclesial times are marked in a spirit of thanks and praise, and for whom the striving for peace and justice is a familiar aspiration. Activities or celebrations related to the great feasts and seasons of the church year could be held in common sometimes, with the children of the various families contributing as age permits. A group of families with children of the same age, for example, might make their Advent wreaths together and also their Advent sharing boxes for the collection of money for the poor, or, just before Lent begins, there might be a joint carnival hour in which dress-up, dance, and fancy treats are enjoyed prior to the austere and solemn Lenten days.

Families could jointly utilize the "cadential" occasions of the church year—the analogy taken from music where cadences punctuate and bring to conclusion the sections of a work. In the liturgical year, the ending of the seasons of Christmas-Epiphany and of the Easter Fifty Days are such times. At these times, the Church completes a liturgical cycle of major importance, even while society at large has anticipated and secularized it (i.e., in the case of Christmas) or is not so much as cognizant of the season (i.e., in the case of the Fifty Days). A small group of families who has kept the spirit of the seasons could come together on these "cadential" occasions to conclude with a flourish what they have observed in their own homes. In this way, children have the supportive presence of both peers and elders who cherish life in Christ and the Church.

Parishes could often be more supportive to the parents of young children who wish to deepen their own spiritual understanding as they pass on the faith tradition to their families. Could the parish arrange for speakers or offer a meeting place or make available to families some resources—books, audio- and video-cassettes, and perhaps the occasional workshop for the whole family? Have parents of young children actually asked, and asked persistently, for the parish's assistance in such an enterprise? Parents themselves must make their parish leaders more aware of the potential for creative action in this little-explored pastoral area. Together, we need to find ways in which we can assist one another in the wonderful and challenging task at hand, nurturing our very young children into a life of praise or, as the psalmist has it, a life filled with new song and festive dance in honor of the Lord.

Suggested Reading

Apostolos-Cappadona, Diane, ed. *The Sacred Play of Children*. New York: Seabury Press, 1983.

Cavalletti, Sofia. *The Religious Potential of the Child*. Patricia M. and Julia M. Coulter, trans.; preface by Mark Searle. Chicago: Liturgy Training Publications, 1992.

Halmo, Joan. *Celebrating the Church Year with Young Children*. Collegeville, Minn.: Liturgical Press; Ottawa, Ont.: Novalis, 1988.

Mueller, Gertrud Nelson. *To Dance with God*. New York: Paulist Press, 1986.

Stewart, Sonja M. and Jerome W. Berryman. *Young Children and Worship*. Louisville, Ky.: Westminster/John Knox Press, 1989.

Notes

1. Sam Keen treats of the relationship between childhood and wonder in *Apology for Wonder* (New York: Harper and Row, 1969), pp. 43-59.

2. Josef Pieper, *Leisure, the Basis of Culture* (London: Faber and Faber, 1963), p. 78.

3. Gail Ramshaw Schmidt, "Readiness for Liturgy: The Formation of Christian Children," *Assembly* 9 (1982): 190.

4. Keen, 201ff.

5. See Edward Hays, *Prayers for the Domestic Church* (Easton, Kans.: Forest of Peace Books, 1979) and Gabe Huck, *A Book of Family Prayer* (New York: Seabury Press, 1979)for extensive collections of occasional prayers. See Sara Wenger Shenk, *Why Not Celebrate!* (Intercourse, Pa.: Good Books, 1987) for a collection of prayers and activities representing the experience of numerous families and a faith community.

6. In the mid-second century, Justin, a lay philosopher and catechist, gave a description of the celebration of the Lord's Day: "On the day which is called Sun-day, all, whether they live in the town or in the country, gather in the same place. Then the memoirs of the apostles or the writings of the prophets are read for as long as time allows. When the reader has finished, the president speaks, exhorting us to live by these noble teachings. Then we rise all together and pray. Then, as we said earlier, when the prayer is

finished, bread, wine and water are brought. The president then prays and gives thanks as well as he can. And all the people reply with the acclamation: Amen! After this the eucharists are distributed and shared out to everyone, and the deacons are sent to take them to those who are absent." *Apologia* 1:67, Lucien Deiss, trans. in *Early Sources of the Liturgy* (Collegeville, Minn.: Liturgical Press, 1967), pp. 25-26.

7. The Council is concerned that "[the rich fare of the Bible] . . . be provided for the faithful at the table of God's word," and that the faithful should be "refreshed at the table of the Lord's body." Second Vatican Council, *Constitution on the Sacred Liturgy* (Rome, 1963), nos. 51 and 48, respectively.

8. Gabe Huck, "Assembly," in *The Sacred Play of Children*, Diane Apostolos-Cappadona, ed. (New York: Seabury Press, 1983), p. 84.

9. Individual books are too numerous to list, but the name of Tomie de Paola must at least be mentioned as an example of an author-illustrator who has created many splendid children's works based on biblical accounts and various other traditional stories.

10. A household might wish to invest in one or two copies of the parish hymnal for their family use. For a fine general musical resource that contains hymns, litanies, and acclamations, both traditional and contemporary, a brief Liturgy of the Hours for morning and evening, and other prayer texts, see *Hymnal for Catholic Students* (Chicago: G.I.A. Publications and Liturgy Training Publications, 1988).

11. For a more detailed historical and scriptural background to the liturgical cycle, see Joan Halmo, *Celebrating the Church Year with Young Children* (Collegeville, Minn.: Liturgical Press; Ottawa, Ont.: Novalis, 1988). This book also includes a selection of simple songs, psalm settings, and acclamations written for families with young children.

12. The fourth-century martyrs of Abitina, *Passio SS. ativi, Saturnini Presbyteri et al.*, in P. F. de Cavalieri, *Note agiografiche*, fasc. 8 (Rome, 1935), 449.

13. Augustine, writing in the early fifth century, describes Christians as an Easter people whose food, drink, and joy forever is "alleluia." See Augustine, Sermon 252,9, Mary Sarah Muldowney, trans. in *Saint Augustine—Sermons on the Liturgical Seasons* (New York: Fathers of the Church, Inc., 1959); *The Fathers of the Church*, Roy Joseph Deferrari, ed., 38:333.

14. Sofia Cavalletti, *The Religious Potential of the Child*, Patricia M. and Julia M. Coulter, trans.; preface by Mark Searle (Chicago: Liturgy Training Publications, 1992), pp. 79ff.

15. John Chrysostom, *Expositio in Psalmum* 41:5,7, in *Patrologia Graeca*, 161 vols. (Paris: D'Amboise, 1857-1866), Jacques Paul Migne, ed., 55:166.

16. Gaynell Cronin, *Sunday throughout the Week* (Notre Dame, Ind.: Ave Maria Press, 1981).

17. For an array of fine "liturgical" recipes along with very interesting historical details regarding traditions of foods for the Church's feasts and seasons, see Evelyn Birge Vitz, *A Continual Feast* (New York: Harper and Row; Toronto: Fitzhenry and Whiteside, 1985).

18. Joseph A. Fiorenza, bishop of Galveston—Houston, *Sunday: The Original Feast Day, A Pastoral Letter on the Sunday Eucharist* (Collegeville, Minn.: Liturgical Press, 1987), p. 27. The issues surrounding the keeping of Sunday in our culture and in our time are also addressed in the brief document *The Meaning of Sunday in a Pluralistic Society* (Ottawa, Ont.: Canadian Conference of Catholic Bishops, 1986).

19. Robert Coles, *The Spiritual Life of Children* (Boston, Mass.: Houghton Mifflin, 1990), p. 171. The boy who made this observation was, of course, not a preschooler, although very young children have an uncanny way of perceiving a great deal more than we suspect.

20. Kathleen and James McGinnis, *Parenting for Peace and Justice* (Maryknoll, N.Y.: Orbis Books, 1981); *Parenting for Peace and Justice: Ten Years Later*, rev. ed. (1990). A book on peace directed specifically to the preschool age is Susanne Wichert, *Keeping the Peace: Practicing Cooperation and Conflict Resolution with Preschoolers* (Santa Cruz, Calif.: New Society Publishers, 1989).

Nurturing Compassion in Children

by Marjorie and Patrick Murray

As a parent, you are the primary role model for your child. How you treat others will often be mirrored by how your child treats others.

Finally, all of you, be of one mind, sympathetic, loving toward one another, compassionate, humble. Do not return evil for evil, or insult for insult, but, on the contrary, a blessing, because to this you were called, that you might inherit a blessing (1 Pt 3:8-9).

The summer before our son, Sean, entered first grade, we went to visit an elderly great-aunt in a nursing home. Our six-year-old transformed within a couple of minutes from an "I want for me" mode of existence into a gracious little boy. Moving down a corridor of very old patients sitting in wheelchairs, there was no hesitancy on his part to risk communicating with those in his path. While we were somewhat discomforted with the scene of helplessness and the smell of disease and old age, he fell behind us in the corridor to stop at each wheelchair. "My name is Sean. What's yours?" Despite the person's struggle to respond, he would continue, "I hope you have a nice day" as he patted their arms and stroked gently their surprised and delighted faces. He just seemed to know that this was the right thing to do. The innocence of his approach, which was totally unsolicited, reinforced for us what we already firmly believed (i.e., it is natural for human beings from an early age to be loving, caring, and compassionate).

Marjorie and Patrick Murray reside in Winter Spring, Florida. She is an early childhood specialist, and he is a parish director of religious education.

Compassion Awakens

Alfie Kohn writes in the March 1991 edition of *Phi Delta Kappan*:

The belief persists in this culture that our darker side is more pervasive, more persistent, and somehow more real than our capacity for what psychologists call *prosocial behavior*. We seem to assume that people are naturally and primarily selfish and will act otherwise only if they are coerced into doing so and carefully monitored. The logical conclusion of this worldview is the assumption that generous and responsible behavior must be forced down the throats of children who would otherwise be inclined to care only about themselves. I believe that it is as natural to help as it is to hurt, that concern for the well-being of others often cannot be reduced to self-interest, that social structures predicated on human selfishness have no claim to inevitability or even prudence.

So it is, within this more positive framework of conviction, that we approach our responsibilities of parenting and education. Time and time again we have been delighted and inspired by the uncomplicated, natural response of children to another's needs. It's true that the early years often reflect a selfish and demanding nature, but this must be attributed to an innate struggle for survival in what must be an often hostile world outside the mother's womb.

It is natural for human beings from an early age to be loving, caring, and compassionate.

To approach the task of formation of our children with the primary focus being to eliminate the negative behavior might very well be a mistake. This is not to say that discipline has no place in the formation of children. Indeed, it has its place from womb to the grave. However, to approach the task that a child is born with a potential perverse human nature that needs our taming process rather than a potentially beautiful God-given nature, which needs to be nurtured and given room to blossom, is to presume that God creates a negative that we mortals must turn into a positive. In reality, nothing is further from the truth.

A baby is born. The baby's every need is catered to by loving, nurturing parents. At the sound of a distressful cry, a bottle is warmed, a diaper is changed, or a rocking chair is put into motion. What moves this helpless human being from the stage of fulfillment of personal needs to fulfillment of the needs of others? How is compassion for others shaped and formed when one's initial existence is solely focused on personal needs?

Have you ever noticed in a nursery of babies that if one cries there is a "contagious" reaction? A baby's earliest response to the needs of others is in the form of global discomfort in reaction to another's distress. As a baby develops into a toddler, this reaction moves from global discomfort to genuine concern demonstrated by patting or touching in response to another's distress. It is moving to see a toddler respond to a mother's sadness or tears by a gentle touch of the face or a pat on the arm.

Another way a young child may respond to distress or need in another is to offer the person in distress the use of whatever is used to comfort the young child. For example, a child has fallen and is crying. The child who is viewing this may run to retrieve his favorite blanket or stuffed animal to give to the distressed child, because that is what gives comfort to him. This is an early expression of compassion and may be reinforced in a young child by verbally acknowledging the response. "Thank you, Jimmy, for helping Brad to feel better by sharing your teddy bear," will help affirm to Jimmy that his response was appropriate prosocial behavior.

As children further develop, they begin to realize that others have unique inner selves with unique needs. As a child's problem-solving ability matures, so does his response to the needs of others. The same child who may have earlier summoned for his distressed friend something of his own to provide comfort, may now acknowledge his friend's personal need and select a method of comfort more appropriate to that need. For example, Jimmy, instead of giving Brad his teddy bear, may now seek Brad's mother or father to provide comfort. As the young child matures in his ability to respond to others, the role of parents, caregivers, and educators is of primary importance.

The Role of Parents

If any credit is to be given to the axiom in religious education circles that "faith is caught, not taught," the same applies to moral values. It is our belief, however, that this is only partially true. Just as there is a need for religious education to make some sense of our faith experience, so, too, we need to educate in moral values to help our children be aware of moral issues and accept responsibility for how they deal with them. Lillian G. Katz, Ph.D., writes in the December 1989 edition of *Parents* magazine:

> [M]oral development is more likely to thrive when parents offer simple explanations of the reasons behind the rules and restrictions rather than moralize, preach, threaten, scold, or punish. Parents who are warm and affectionate seem to strengthen their children's desire to meet expectations for ethical behavior. When moral transgressions do inevitably occur, it is best to address them immediately and directly and not to belabor them. Suggestions about how to resist the same temptation next time can put the incident in a constructive light and reinforce the reasoning behind the prohibition. For example, if your child deliberately hits another child, tell him/her that the next time he/she feels angry he/she can come to you and that there are better ways to express anger.

It is by education that conscience is formed. A child's natural capacity to comfort and nurture is developed into mature compassion and charitable expressions when the reason for it becomes more evident. This also enables a discernment of guilt or remorse when there is failure to express the moral value. That's how conscience works. To enable children to know what guilt or remorse is may be touching a sensitive nerve in some, but without a balanced conscience, there won't be a true understanding of the value of prosocial behavior. Children grasp at an early age what is right and what is wrong. But without knowing reasons for their decision, they may very well lose the initiative to use good judgment. It is then that reactions become selfish and self-centered and values become based on what primarily seems good to them at that time. The reasons a child might give for exercising a good moral value may not necessarily be an adult reason. Most often, it is the simplest reason of all (i.e., the person helped, nurtured, or comforted just needed help)! When our son, Sean, was queried about why he was so kind to the people in the nursing home, he responded, "Because I wanted to!" Why did he want to? "Because it made them smile!"

No thought process here of good Christian behavior or that the Scriptures call us to be loving and kind. That will all come in time. For Sean, it was enough to see another person smile. The smile was the reason to do it. We reinforced his actions by assuring him it was good to try to make others happy and that we were very proud of him! We must eventually be ready for the inevitable questions of old age, illness, and loneliness. A child's ability to understand levels of compassion and reasons for expressing compassion grows and develops as the child grows and develops.

We believe the Church must do more to be on the front line in establishing a nurturing model for early childhood.

A phrase that is used frequently in today's society where both parents have careers is, "It's not the quantity of time, but the quality of time that really matters." It salves the conscience of busy parents who must send their children at an early age to day-care centers. Both of us have careers, and we, too, go through the guilt processes that we don't spend enough time with our children. Children demand a lot of time and individual attention. We know that the amount of time spent with the children is of paramount importance. So to compensate, there has to be sacrifice in other areas, such as social and recreational time spent as a couple. This often puts tremendous stress on a marital relationship. During that time, the role model of parents as nurturing each other, as well as the children, is what ultimately determines the emotional expression and values response of the child as he or she matures.

We hear much today about child abuse. This is usually thought of in terms of physical or sexual abuse. Far more insidious today, however, is the emotional maltreatment or neglect of children, where there is failure to provide love, nurturing, bonding, and security—all things a child needs for health and happiness. In the September 1991 issue of *U.S. Catholic,* Jean Guarino writes:

Child neglect occurs at all income levels and in all social classes. It can be seen among children in *gilded ghettos* whose parents are too affluent for a child's good, parents who give the child everything but attention and measure out what they are pleased to call *quality time* in dribs and drabs. Child neglect is also widespread among impoverished families and in homes where one or both parents are depressed, ill, preoccupied by financial problems, alcoholic, or simply too young to have any idea of how to nurture children.

This latter category is particularly startling since we have an increasing number of children who are "the children of children" who themselves are in the predicament because they were emotionally neglected.

Jim Egan, a Washington, D.C., clinical psychologist says:

Children are like computers in that what goes in, comes out, and each child gets only one floppy disk. There is a critical period in the development of every infant: the merry-go-round goes around only once, and the infant does or does not get the brass ring or the full enjoyment of the potential that was his or her birthright. By the time the child reaches school age, it is usually too late to undo the damage of this early neglect.

Therefore, if you are to nurture your child to show compassion at an early age, you must begin with birth. The role of parents is vital. As a parent, what you say and do in your daily interaction with your family plays a leading role in whether your child, born with a natural desire to care for others, will grow up to be a caring adult. Take a moment to assess mentally what your child hears you say or watches you do in the course of a day or a week. Do you communicate with sincere interest and respect? Are you sensitive to the feelings of others in your family or do you strip their feelings and dignity with harsh and cutting words or tone of voice? How does your child see and hear you interact with friends, acquaintances, store clerks, or strangers you may encounter? Remember, as a parent, you are the primary role model for your child. How you treat others will often be mirrored by how your child treats others.

We believe a child's natural desire to care for others is very strong. Parents are important keys to the fulfillment of that desire. God knows we are not ready for canonization as parents. The problems of every household are there in our home, too. Our four-year-old is just as likely to bite or scratch the six-year-old, and the screams of "it's mine" are just as prevalent. But we know, too, that while we keep working at being nurturing and compassionate adults, there are signs that our little ones are reflecting that model in so many different beautiful ways.

The Role of Day Care

While most will agree that the development of moral values, compassion, and concern for others ought to be the primary responsibility of parents, it is also true that it is not to be found in all homes. Sometimes, day-care centers and classrooms are a child's only positive experience toward the development of compassion and concern for others. Conversely, a child's experience outside of the home may easily negate the positive model in the home. More and more children, from an early age, spend most of their waking hours in day-care centers, preschool, and then regular school. These settings need to either provide what some children may not otherwise be receiving or reinforce the positive experiences children are receiving in their home environment. Alfie Kohn also writes:

> If we had to pick a logical setting in which to guide children toward caring about, empathizing with, and helping other people, it would be a place where they would regularly come in contact with their peers and where some sort of learning is already taking place. The school is such an obvious choice that one wonders how it could be that the active encouragement of prosocial behavior—apart from occasional exhortations to be polite—plays no part in the vast majority of American classrooms.

He goes on to reflect that this probably stems from a nervousness "that an agenda concerned with social and moral issues amounts to teaching values—a dangerous business for a public institution."

True! But to do nothing about prosocial values in these settings is to, by implication at least, instill a negative set of values. What is wrong with teaching our children not only to think, but also to care? The end result must necessarily be a less violent generation. When addressing issues of discipline and teacher/student communication, the courses offered in teacher and day-care worker training fall short. They concentrate almost solely on "the letter of the law" rather than concentrating on the importance of loving and nurturing the children. The "lip service" is there, but educators are terrified lest their caring response to a child be sadly misconstrued. Care must be given to the selection process of those in charge of our children. Credentials are important, but innate empathy is also important, particularly when selecting day-care and preschool workers. It is an awesome responsibility to place such tender young minds and hearts in the care of others at a time when children are more naturally with their parents in the home environment. Those who, on a daily basis, take the place of a parent must supply the nurturing model of home and school at a very critical age. By the time a child is ready for kindergarten, the formation is firmly in place.

If a parent must place a child in the hands of others during these formative years, then there is a responsibility on the part of the parent to know as much as possible about who is caring for the child. Also, it is important to know how a child is being cared for. To assist in making this determination, a parent must spend time observing in the center or classroom noting the interaction between the staff and the children. Are the staff responsive to the emotional and physical needs of the children?

The Role of the Church

We believe the Church must do more to be on the front line in establishing a nurturing model for early childhood. In Mark 9:36-37,42, Jesus sets the standard. He speaks of welcoming a child and in doing so one welcomes Jesus. Then he goes on to warn strongly against giving scandal to a child. An ever-increasing number of urban and suburban parishes in the United States are establishing day-care and early childhood learning centers. They proliferate even in parishes that have no Catholic schools. Dig deep enough, and one will find that, even here, profit is the bottom line. Church day-care workers are paid minimum wages and frequently kept on part-time status so no benefits need to be paid on their behalf. Few, if any, diocesan guidelines have been established for such centers. Churches accept preschoolers in far greater numbers than they do in Catholic schools, yet there are no diocesan or national offices or policies in place. This is a travesty! Most of these church centers operate entirely on state guidelines.

Opportunities are being lost to bring to this tender age group what it means to love and be loved in the model of the Good Shepherd. This is not to say that the majority of people in church day-care centers are uncaring people. Our own experience has been quite the opposite; we have been blessed. However, we must be honest and admit that good service for working parents is the primary goal rather than to "teach as Jesus taught." There is no training provided by the Church, although it is provided by the state. Minimum wage or part-time positions do not always attract the most committed worker. The whole notion of ministry is being completely overlooked by the Church in this critical area.

Statistically, the largest enrollment for religious education falls into the early childhood range. Three- and four-year-old programs, kindergarten, first and second grades are usually the largest classes. Yet, so few of our religious educators have any early childhood training. If there is validity in providing trained youth ministers for our teenagers, why not trained early childhood specialists for the largest religious education group? Catholic publishers have made strides in providing religious education materials for preschoolers but more is needed, especially tactile materials. Often, too much is left to the inventiveness of the volunteer catechist who may find a lack of suitable resources.

*If you are to nurture your child to show
compassion at an early age,
you must begin at birth.*

A vast bureaucratic church may often be perceived by a child as distant, unloving, and lacking compassion. Imagine the young child who becomes restless during a church service. This natural tendency is most often not met with compassion and understanding, but with impatience, disapproval, even anger—both from the parents and the church community. There is no tolerance, as a rule, for early childhood to share in any liturgical experience. While babies at baptism may be "cute," they quickly get the message that they are not always welcome around the eucharistic table.

What would Jesus do? Again read Mark, chapter 9. Perhaps, more "scandal" can be perceived than "welcome." Let's face it! We are not always a model of a nurturing, compassionate community. And yet, we expect to have a role in the lives of the children and often wonder why many children turn to violence rather than have their natural compassionate and nurturing traits developed.

In summary, then, for the context of this article, we propose these few reflections:

- As parents, we must set the model of love, nurturing, and compassion.

- Our children are given to us by God with innate capabilities of nurturing and compassion. These can be thwarted by bad example and lack of time spent by parents and others in developing natural characteristics.

- Great care must be given to the choice of caregiver when it comes to the selection of day-care centers or early childhood learning centers.

- The Church must inevitably address its ministry to children in this age group and increase its involvement and direction when it comes to being a nurturing "Mother Church" for its youngest members.

Suggested Reading

Firestone, Robert. *Compassionate Childrearing: An In-depth Approach to Optimal Parenting.* Insight Books, 1990.

Guarino, Jean. "Sharp Words Hurt More Than a Slap in the Face." *U.S. Catholic* (September 1991).

Kantrowitz, Barbara and Pat Wingert. "Teaching Charity to Children." *Newsweek* (January 1, 1990): 41.

Katz, Lillian G. "Beginners Ethics." *Parents* (December 1989): 213.

Kohn, Alfie. "Caring Kids: The Role of the Schools." *Phi Delta Kappan* (March 1991): 496-506.

Smith, Charles A. "Nurturing Kindness Through Storytelling." *Young Children* (September 1986): 46-51.

Weissbound, Bernice. "How Children Learn to Care." *Parents* (August 1991): 128.

From Our House to Yours, Reading with Our Children: When, What, Why

by Betsy and Al Puntel

The Christian story, told wisely and gently, inviting storyteller and child to become part of the story of God's love, creates a bond of love among the child, the storyteller, and God, which can become a lasting treasure.

Storytelling

Storytelling is part of every human culture. "In the beginning was the Word" (Jn 1)—and words and stories are one of our greatest gifts. Before the human family had books, it had stories. Before our children come to the fullness of enjoying storybooks, they can enjoy stories. Song–games that involve playing with a baby, such as "Incey Wincey Spider"; nursery rhymes and songs; name games such as "Grandma went to market and brought . . . "; and nighttime homespun tales are just some of these "stories."

Increasingly, however, the use of books for enjoyment and storytelling from babyhood on up is becoming a shared value. Reflecting on the value of books and storytelling can impact on our children's human and spiritual development, on the parent-child relationship, and on the quality of life in the home.

Betsy and Al Puntel live with their six children in Philadelphia. She is a religious educator and he is a high school teacher.

What Stories? The "Bad News"

Such reflection is necessary, because words can be deadly. Today, we can turn on commercial television and quickly see that not all "stories" are worth our children's time. In fact, it is indicative of the poverty of our children's culture that so much storytelling has been delegated to the television and to the sitcom. Getting away from this addiction and making a responsible judgment about storytelling in our home is an important aspect of the "ministry" of parents, who help bring life to the life we give our children. Especially when our children are young, we want to give them a taste for the good in stories as well as in food! Even more than making sure that junk food is not a staple of their diets, we should make sure that "junk" stories are not, either.

Libraries: The "Good News"

It is good news that there is, within most of our neighborhoods, a public library. In it can be found many storybooks to enrich our children's growing up. Parents, teachers, and religious educators can reclaim the "story" as an important, integral dimension of the Christian upbringing we promised our children when we shared with them the great grace of baptism. This is a grace that is meant to permeate each aspect of their (and our) growing and being. It is a God-with-us grace to fill days and nights, hopes and dreams, imaginations and intelligence, play and work, loving and fearing, wondering and exploring. Another "ministry" of great importance could be the development of the books and resources of the neighborhood or parish library to aid this kind of growing.

Reference Books

There are several excellent anthologies of the "best" in children's books. What we will try to add is a prospective on what's available in terms of baptism's holistic grace—a grace that is as holistic as the commandments to "love God with our whole hearts and minds and souls and strength" and "to love our neighbor as ourselves."

What to Look for:
Secular and Religious

It has been part of the Catholic genius to take the bread and wine of human life and to make it holy. That is what we will do here, too: take secular books that offer us a means of bringing to the child the "bread and wine" of human life, thus strengthening their own good growing. The stories we share broaden and strengthen and prepare the way for the hearing, understanding, and living of the Christian story. We will also list some of what we have found to be the best in Christian story. To do this, we have chosen to list stories according to categories: family life stories; friends and neighbors stories; childhood stories (to build self-esteem by developing understanding); stories that strengthen the good: work stories, stories highlighting sacramental symbols, stories highlighting sacramental actions.

Within the list, authors whose works have religious themes will be denoted by an asterisk (*). Nonreligious stories may sometimes lead to the storyteller's additions of religious dimensions. This may be done as a prayer or as part of the story-experience.

How to Use the List

The list at the end of this essay is not exhaustive, but it is indicative of what you might want to look for as you browse through your library or bookstore in search of a book to read or buy for that special child (or group of children). We think the categories are helpful guides for that search. So are librarians!

When to Start Reading Books to Your Child

A child is never too young for a story or for a book. Even babies love books! The cadence of the parent's voice, the sound of the language, the pictures, the laptime—even if just for a minute here or there—are a real treat. As the baby grows and begins to chew on everything (even on their very own board books), the parent continues to cultivate a "taste" for books in the child, and the child soon grows to enjoy the stories and pictures and laptime and eventually gives up eating the books!

Creating Story-Sharing Rituals

Bedtime has always been a favorite time for telling stories. We have found that once parents and children get hooked on reading together, myriads of other possibilities open up. Getting to the library often; giving and receiving books as gifts; telling stories at bedtime, quiet times, vacation times; choosing books for family sharing (maybe as part of Sunday's holiness? family night?); and searching for just the right book to help a child with a certain difficulty or challenge. This is good, cheap, fun, and constitutive of being a family that shares a story. To emphasize, there is probably a book on every childhood challenge—search and you will find a story, or at least the love and wisdom and courage to make one up. We have tried to be broad in our approach, but many topics (e.g., having an alcoholic parent or a chronically ill sibling) we have not touched. Ask the librarian for help.

The Christian Story

The Christian story is one that your child will be glad to hear. Told wisely and gently, inviting storyteller and child to become part of the story of God's love, Christian storytelling creates a bond of love among the child, the storyteller, and God, which can become a lasting treasure. We include a sampling of books, tapes, and videos for such sharing, as well as a model for sharing stories within the faith community and beyond the home/family setting.

It is indicative of the poverty of our children's culture that so much storytelling has been delegated to the television and to the sitcom.

In the Parish

In religious education, story hours can include whole families, children of varying ages, or parents with little ones. Borrowing from a secular model in neighborhood libraries, church story hours can give credibility and life to the telling of the Christian story, especially when the story hour includes parents with their children. Then, telling the story becomes part of living the story, which is what it's all about. Also in religious education sessions, stories can illuminate a gospel value.

Bibliotherapy

Bibliotherapy describes the use of books for the healing of life's hurts. Stories that allow children to know they are not alone in grieving, in being lonely or afraid or angry or in pain are very helpful. Also, humorous stories that gently accept the human condition are beneficial. Some people are trained in bibliotherapy, and there are resources in your library for your own research into this area.

Repetition

Children may ask for the same book over and over until parents become very tired of it. It's an act of love to be patient with a child's need for repetition. Your child will work through whatever the book is about for him or her, and a time will come when you might even ask the child if you could *please* read that book one more time.

Teachable, Readable Moments

Reading storybooks at home could be preparatory for the next week's Scripture readings at church or a follow-up for the previous week. We parents ordinarily observe what our children enjoy in books and choose for them or help them choose what to bring home to read. Building on our observations, we can use our creativity to teach our children much about the world. It is hoped that they are already having a chance to observe from living life with us. We can do this without violating our children's integrity or spontaneous exploration of their world.

For example, if a small child is interested in dinosaurs, *Derek, the Knitting Dinosaur* by Blackwood (Carol Rhoda) is about a peaceable dinosaur, who spends its time knitting to clothe the naked. Or, if interested in animal stories in general, what about the classic story by Leaf and Lawson, *Ferdinand* (Viking/Puffin)? Ferdinand is a peaceable bull who likes to smell the flowers, and the book has simple, charming drawings in colors attractive even to infants. Another animal story with "peace and justice" overtones is Jackson's *The Tawny Scrawny Lion* (Golden Books/Western Publishing), about an enemy who becomes a friend by the innocence of a small rabbit who lures a hungry lion to share the rabbit's "alternate" diet. *The Banza* by Marc Brown (Dial) is again about animals, about friends and enemies, and music and has colorful illustrations worth looking at in their own right. *Marie, Louise, and Christopher* by Carison (Scribners) and the *Frog and Toad* books by Lobel (Harper and Row) are animal stories about friendship. The former is specifically about a reconciliation; the latter stories have many themes and are a definite *must* as modern-day parables. The *Amanda Pig* and *Oliver Pig* stories by Van Leeuwen and illustrated by Lobel (Dial) are likewise gems, with many family themes.

Teaching and Parenting with Books

To elaborate on the *teaching* that parents can do with stories, some studies have shown that parents who take time after or during the reading of a story to ask questions and to allow their children to ask questions in return have more proficient readers on their hands later in childhood than do parents who simply read the stories. So, pulling out some of the meaning and events and opinions about the story—again, in ways that respect the child's integrity and spontaneous curiosities—makes good sense for the child's reading readiness.

Since conflict and division are so much a part of the human experience, we choose to elaborate a bit more on the theme of "peaceableness and reconciliation," moving now beyond the animal stories into other stories that build a child's treasure of experiences of this grace in life. *Atuk* by Dimjan (North-South Books) is about an Eskimo boy whose search for vengeance leads to a dead end, and he finds his *peace* in being peaceable. *The Hurt* by Doleski (Paulist) has a similar theme, with a simple story line and drawings. *I Hate My Brother Harry* (Harper and Row) is a story of a sibling with very angry feelings about a bossy big brother, but it's also a story of the possibility of a new relationship because of the presence of a deep-down seed of mutual love. Hazen's *Even If I Did Something Awful* (Atheneum) depicts a faithful mother's love that can overcome any evil; M. W. Brown's classic *The Runaway Bunny* (Harper and Row; also available in pudgy board book) with its charming drawings and story has a similar theme and is a must for any library or home. Cazet's *You Make the Angels Cry* (Bradbury) also tells a story resounding in the faithfulness of the love offered even the most errant of the naughty. *Peter Rabbit* by Potter (F. Warne and Co.) is another classic about a naughty rabbit who takes the consequences but is always welcome back home. *Fire Cat* by Averill (Harper and Row) is about a naughty cat whose conversion comes in finding the right job and who finds he needs to do penance for past misdeeds. It is an excellent story with simple art. These kinds of stories build self-esteem and even give parent and child a chance to make up after an altercation.

In religious education, story hours can include whole families, children of varying ages, as well as adults.

Then, there are the books about parents and our need to make up. *The Quarreling Book* is one. Van Woerkom's *The Queen Who Couldn't Bake Gingerbread* (Knopf), illustrated by Galdone, is a treasure of a tale about marriage and about making up. Children struggling to reconcile within themselves the pain of their parents' failure at marriage might appreciate Stinson's *Mom and Dad Don't Live Together Anymore* (Firefly) and Christiansen's *My Mother's House, My Father's House* (Atheneum). The first has a theme of acceptance and grieving; the second is a story of a child's hope and love and personal integration in the face of her parents' separation. A child who has been abused in some way might find a story a helpful way to begin to talk about his or her deepest hurts. Buckley's *Chilly Stomach* (Harpercrest) is only one of many such books. Yashima's *The Emperor and the Kite* (Viking) is the story of a daughter's loyalty to her unappreciative and unloving father and his change of heart.

Books that follow themes from the Scriptures are good to buy for the home and for the church library. *The Lost Son's House* in the Building Series (Moody) is a board book shaped like a house that tells the story of the merciful father and the prodigal son. Doney's *The 99th Sheep* (Tyndale) explicates the reconciliation and fidelity themes in that parable; while Iguchi's timeless *The Tiny Sheep* (Judson Press) is a classic retelling of the Good Shepherd story, complete with Iguchi's lovely illustrations. Dumell's *The Lord's Prayer* (Roman, Inc.) with its photo-style art is an introduction to this prayer, with emphasis on forgiving and being forgiven. As a child gets to the other side of the fifth birthday, Carr's *God, I Need to Talk to You About . . .* series, including the topics of paying attention, lying, cheating, bad temper, sharing, and hurting others (Concordia), is a very good series. Walters' compilation of Scripture and daily-life stories in *Forgiving One Another* (Ave Maria Press) is similarly recommended for that age. Finally, deKort's *Zacchaeus* (Augsburg) from his highly commendable series of Bible stories, has fine art and simple text, making it a perfect choice for children.

Book List

At the end of this article, we've listed stories about family relationships and friendships; stories that begin to illuminate the deep human meanings of sacramental symbols; stories about work; stories about daily life. Certainly, we don't envision giving children courses in stories according to these topics. We chose the topics after some thought and prayer, and we chose the books accordingly. We offer this list as a resource to aid your search for "the right book at the right time," not necessarily as a comprehensive listing but as a springboard. Books mentioned in our preceding essay are not repeated in the list.

Conclusion

How might one use the list that follows? Suppose that you are expecting another child. You might look in the "sibling" section and find some books you'd like to share with your child. Each entry gives a two- or three-word clue as to the theme of the book; also included is a rough idea of what ages would appreciate the story line. We highly recommend that, after perhaps sharing with your children some of the books we suggest, you learn how to use the resources in your own local library. Ask the librarian how to look up children's books according to subject, author, or title. He or she can also help you find publishers' addresses, should you want to order a book directly.

Suppose you are trying to help your child understand the Mass. A book such as *The Legend of Bluebonnet* by dePaola is a beautiful story about the fruitfulness of a sacrifice, and Galdone's *The Little Red Hen* is a classic about the dimension of mutual service and table fellowship. Both have outstanding art, too. Even before our children are ready for such "big" stories, books such as Greeley's *Where's My Share?* coupled with the experience of sharing family mealtime, are great for building "eucharist readiness." Any pre-seven child is little: sharing the story's meaning has to happen in little ways, some at the reading of the story, and some by drawing comparisons later. Parents are in that special place that can personalize for our children the sharing of the stories, particularly if we are in that place with God!

Stories Suggested for Children

[The following books are listed by author, title, publisher, age group best-suited, and themes reflected. Authors whose works have religious themes are denoted by an asterisk.]

Alexander, L. *The King's Fountain* (Dutton). Age 3 and up. Self-worth and social justice.

Brown. *Wait Till the Moon Is Full* (Harper and Row). Age 3 and up. Waiting.

Burton. *The Little House* (Houghton Mifflin). Age 4 and up. Change; self-acceptance.

dePaola. *Francis: The Poor Man of Assisi* (Holiday House). Age 4 and up. Freedom; love of God. and *The Legend of the Bluebonnet* (Putnam). Age 4 and up. Sacrifice.

Erickson and Raffi. *I'll Try* (Viking Kestrel). Age 2 and up. Perseverance.

Freeman, D. *Dandelion* (Viking). Age 3 and up. Loved as is; vanity.

Fujikawa. *Fairy Tales and Fables* (Grosset and Dunlap). Age 3 and up. Many and varied.

Galdone. *The Wise Fool* (Random House). Age 3 and up. Humor; justice.

Gauch and de DePaola. *The Little Friar Who Flew* (Putnam). Age 3 and up. Joy in God; creation.

Greene. *A Hole in the Dike* (Crowell). Age 3 and up. Danger; courage.

Hale and dePaola. *Mary Had a Little Lamb* (Holiday House). Age 2 and up. Care returned.

Klug. *Christian Family Bedtime Stories* (Augsburg). Age 3 and up. Many and varied; Christian.

LaFontaine. *The Miller, the Boy, and the Donkey* (Watts). Age 3 and up. Conscience; peer pressure.

Lionel. *Swimmy* (Pantheon). Age 3 and up. Community.

McDermott. *The Stone-Cutter* (Viking). Age 4 and up. Envy; power; contentment.

Ness. *Sam, Bangs, and Moonshine* (H. R. & W.). Age 4 and up. Fantasy; reality; lying.

Otsuka. *Suho and the White Horse* (Viking). Age 4 and up. Love/death of pet/remembering.

Platti. *The Happy Owls* (Atheneum). Age 3 and up. Thankfulness.

Roop. *Keep the Lights Burning, Abbie* (Carol Rhoda). Age 3 and up. Courage.

Dr. Seuss. *The Lorax* (Random House). Age 3 and up. Ecology.

Silverstein. *The Giving Tree* (Harper and Row). Age 4 and up. Selfless giving.

Sparrow King. *Nathanael the Grublet* (Candle Co.). Age 4 and up. Stealing; salvation. (Also on tape from Cherry River Music Co.)

Steig. *Brave Irene* (FSG). Age 4 and up. Love; courage.

Zemach. *The Judge* (FSG). Age 3 and up. Witnessing to the truth. Also *It Could Always Be Worse* (FSG). Age 3 and up. Thankful/grumbling faith.

Siblings

Doney. *Now We Have a New Baby* (Winston Windows). Age 2 and up. New baby.

Hoban. *A Birthday for Frances* (Macmillan). Age 3 and up. Sibling rivalry. Also *A Baby Sister for Frances* (Macmillan). Age 3 and up. New baby. Also *The Arthur Stories* (Harper Trophy). Age 3 and up. Many titles.

Keats, E. J. *Peter's Chair* (Harper and Row). Age 2 and up. New baby.

Naylor. *The Baby, the Bed and the Rose* (Clarion). Age 2 and up. Sibling's love.

Zolotow. *Big Sister and Little Sister* (Harper and Row). Age 2 and up. Sister love.

Fathers

Baum. *I Want to See the Moon* (Overlook Press). Age 2 and up. Wonder.

Bunting. *No Nap!* (Clarion). Age 3 and up. Dad falls asleep.

Caines, J. *Daddy* (Harper and Row). Age 3 and up. Divorced, caring Dad.

Hines. *Daddy Makes the Best Spaghetti* (Clarion). Age 3 and up. Day with Dad.

Zolotow. *A Father Like That. . . .* (Harper and Row). Age 3 and up. Fatherless child. Also *That Summer Night* (HarperCollins). Age 3 and up. Sharing wonder.

Mothers

Baum. *After Dark* (Overlook Press). Age 2 and up. Waiting for Mom.

Cresswell. *Trouble* (Dutton). Age 4 and up. Mother as a child.

dePaola. *La Nuestra Senora de Guadalupe* (also in English [Holiday House]). Age 4 and up. America's May; the poor.

Eastman. *Are You My Mother?* (Random House). Age 2 and up. Seeking/finding.

Godden. *A Kindle of Kittens* (Viking). Age 4 and up. Mother's care; adoption.

Jarrell. *The Knee Baby* (Farrar, Straus, Giroux). Age 3 and up. New baby—both loved.

Mursch. *Love You Forever* (Firefly). Age 3 and up. Mother/son: birth to death.

Wells. *Hazel's Amazing Mother* (Dial). Age 3 and up. Humor.

Williams. *A Chair for My Mother* (Greenwillow). Age 3 and up. Single parent; solidarity.

Zolotow. *Some Things Go Together* (Harper and Row). Age 2 and up. Mother/child.

Family

Allard. *The Stupids. . . .* (Houghton Mifflin). Age 4 and up. Humor. Several in series.

Caines. *Abby* (Harpercrest). Age 2 and up. Adoption.

Caudill. *A Certain Small Shepherd* (Dell). Age 5 and up. Hospitality; handicap.

Eastman. *The Best Nest* (Beginners). Age 2 and up. Content with one's home.

Glen. *Ruby* (Putnam). Age 3 and up. Handicap; adoption.

Hazen and Hayman. *Tight Times* (Viking Kestrel). Age 3 and up. Unemployment.

Hendershot. *In Coal Country* (Knopf). Age 4 and up. Coal country.

Lobel. *One More Mouse to Feed* (Harper and Row). Age 2 and up. Solidarity in need.

McCloskey. *Make Way for Ducklings* (Puffin). Age 3 and up. Homing.

Polacco. *The Keeping Quilt* (Simon and Schuster). Age 4 and up. Family roots.

Ringgold. *Tar Beach* (Crown). Age 3 and up. Poor folks' roof-top vacation.

Sendak. *Pierre: A Cautionary Tale* (Harper Trophy). Age 3 and up. Obedience; caring.

Steig. *Sylvester and the Magic Pebble* (Simon and Schuster). Age 4 and up. Return to family.

Winter. *The Bear and the Fly* (Crown). Age 3 and up. It's not always easy; humor. Also *The Drinking Gourd* (Knopf). Age 3 and up.

Grandparents

Aliki. *The Two of Them* (Harper and Row). Age 4 and up. Death.

Brooks. *Timothy and Gramps* (Bradbury). Age 3 and up. Friend making.

dePaola. *Now One Foot, Now the Other* (Greenwillow). Age 3 and up. Needing assistance.

Griffiths. Georgia Music (Greenwillow). Age 4 and up. Depression.remembering.

Stevenson. *What's Under My Bed?* (Puffin). Age 3 and up. Help with fear of the dark.

Zolotow. *My Grandson Lew* (Harper and Row). Age 2 and up. Death.

Grandmothers

Bartolli. *Nonna* (Haney House). Age 3 and up. Death.

Bunting. *The Wednesday Surprise* (Clarion). Age 3 and up. Grandma learns to read.

dePaola. *Nana Upstairs, Nana Downstairs* (Holiday House). Age 3 and up. Death.

Hines. *Grandma Gets Grumpy* (Clarion). Age 3 and up. Tuckered Grandma.

Miles. *Annie and the Old One* (Little, Brown). Age 4 and up. Death; Native America.

Nelson. *Always Gramma* (Putnam). Age 4 and up. Granny with Alzheimer's disease.

Williams. *Music, Music for Everyone* (Greenwillow). Age 4 and up. Sick Granny; solidarity.

Zolotow. *William's Doll* (Harper and Row). Age 3 and up. Grandma understands.

Childhood

[The following list is only a small sampling of stories for building self-acceptance, self-esteem, and understanding; and for building language and vocabulary skills. Also, inquire at your local library for the "toddler" section, which will have numerous books relating to these topics.]

Alexander. *How My Library Grew* (Wilson). Age 4 and up. Getting a library card.

Baker, S. A. *The Stormy Night* (Tyndal). Age 3 and up. Psalms; fear of the dark.

Brown, Marc. *Arthur's Eyes* (L. B. Company). Age 3 and up. Glasses.

Brown. *Goodnight Moon* (Harper and Row). Age 3 and up. Baby and nighttime.

Clark. *In My Mother's House* (Viking). Age 5 and up. Native American daily.

deKort. *Jesus and the Storm* (Augsburg). Age 2 and up. Jesus and fear/faith.

dePaola. *The Cloud Book* (Holiday House). Age 3 and up. Clouds.

Doney. *Now I Am Big; When I Was Little* (Winston Windows). Age 2 and up. Growing up.

Dragonwagon. *Will It Be Okay?* (Harper and Row). Age 4 and up. Reassurance; common fears.

Fitzgerald, Annie. *Dear God. . . .* (many books in the series [Augsburg]). Age 3 and up. Everyday events.

Florian. *A Winter Day* (Greenwillow). Age 1 and up. Winter events.

Ginsburg. *The Sun's Asleep Behind the Hill* (Greenwillow). Age 1 and up. Sleeptime.

Graham. *The Red Woolen Blanket* (Little, Brown). Age 2 and up. Security blanket.

Gray and Dupasquier. *A Country Far Away* (Watts-Orchard). Age 2 and up. Multicultural.

Greenfield. *Nathaniel Talking* (Black Butterfly). Age 5 and up. Inner city.

Hill. *Evan's Corner* (Holt, Rinehart, Winston). Age 4 and up. Small house; big family. Also *Spot Books* series. Flap books.

Hirsh, Retold. *Joseph, Who Loved the Sabbath* (Wiking Kestrel). Age 4 and up. Sunday/Sabbath.

Hoban. *Bedtime for Frances* (Harper Trophy). Age 3 and up. Bedtime.

Impey and Porter. *A Letter to Santa Claus* (Delacorte). Age 4 and up. Surprise; giving and receiving.

Keats. *Whistle for Willie* (Puffin). Age 3 and up. Learning to whistle.

Krasilovsky. *The Very Tall/Small Little Girl* (H. M.). Age 4 and up. Affirming as is.

Milne. *When We Were Very Young* (Dutton/Dell). Age 4 and up. Fantasy vignettes.

Murphy. *God Cares When I . . .* (David C. Cook). Age 3 and up. God's word in my heart; psalms.

Musgrove.*Ashanti to Zulu* (African Tradition Dial). Age 3 and up. ABC; African life; lonely art.

Panek. *Ba Ba Sheep Wouldn't Go to Sleep* (Watts Orchard). Age 1 and up. Need for sleep.

Raskin. *Spectacles* (Atheneum). Age 4 and up. Accepts need for glasses.

Reeves. *Thank You God for . . .* (Judson Press). Age 2 and up. Thankfulness series.

Rogers, F. *Going to Daycare; . . . Dentist*; etc. (Putnam). Age 2 and up. Dealing with "new" experiences.

Ross. *The Little Quiet Book* (Random House). Age 1 and up. Nursery rhymes.

Singer. *Nine O'Clock Lullaby* (HarperCollins). Age 3 and up. Multicultural, daily.

Showers. *The Listening Walk* (HarperCollins). Age 3 and up. Read and do it. Also *How Many Teeth?* (HarperCollins). Age 3 and up. Losing teeth.

Walt Disney. *Happy Healthy Pooh Book* (Western). Age 4 and up. Health in mind and body.

Williams. *More, Moore Says the Baby* (Greenwillow). Age infant up. Games baby loves.

Wilkins. *Prayers for a Small Child* (Random House). Age 2 and up. Prayers.

Zolotow. *The Sky Was Blue* (Harper and Row). Age 4 and up. Child's/Mom's/Grandma's childhood. Also *Something Is Going to Happen* (Harpercrest). Age 3 and up. Daily; snow is coming. Also *Summer Is . . .* (Crowell). Age 3 and up. Summer experiences. Also *When the Wind Stops* (Harpercrest). Age 3 and up. Questions; life experiences.

Tapes/Records

Landry.* "Hola Dios" (I and II). Age infant and up. Also available in English.

Miffleton.* "Wake Up the Earth Baby." Age infant and up.

Raffi.* "Beluga." Age infant and up.

Friends and Neighbors

Aliki. *We Are Best Friends* (Greenwillow). Age 3 and up. Friend moves away; new friend.

Anglund. *A Friend Is Someone Who Likes You* (Harper Trophy). Age 3 and up. A friend.

Bonsall. *It's Mine* (Harper and Row). Age 3 and up. Greed; sharing.

Briggs. *The Snowman* (Random House). Video. Age 3 and up. Friendship loss.

Cohn. *I Had a Friend Named Peter . . .* (Morrow). Age 3 and up. Friend's death.

Ets. *Play with Me* (Viking). Age 3 and up. Nature; animals; being quiet.

Freeman. *Corduroy* (Viking). Age 3 and up. Choosing; stuffed bear story; classic for children.

Fujikawa. *Welcome Is a Wonderful Word* (Gosset and Dunlap). Age 2 and up. New neighbors.

Ginsburg. *The Chick and the Duckling* (Macmillan). Age 1 and up. Love for another; love of self.

Gruelle. *Raggedy Ann and Andy* series (Viking). Age 5 and up. Kindness; being brave and selfless.

Hebblethwaite.* *My Secret Life (a Friendship with God)* (Morehouse). Age 4 and up. Excellent book on praying alone with God.

Heide. *That's What Friends Are For* (Four Winds). Age 4 and up. Kindness.

Joslin. *What Do You Do, Dear?* (Harper Trophy). Age 3 and up. Manners.

Lionni. *Little Blue and Little Yellow* (Astor). Age 4 and up. Love and acceptance.

Marbach.* *Saints for All Seasons* (St. Anthony Messenger Press). Age 4 and up. Jesus' friends.

Marshall. *What's the Matter with Carruthers?* (Houghton Mifflin). Age 3 and up. Patient understanding. Also *George and Martha* series (Houghton Mifflin). Age 3 and up. Humor.

Parry.* *The Beginning* (Augsburg). Age 1 and up. Creation.

Sharmat. *Gladys Told Me to Meet Her Here* (Harper and Row). Age 4 and up. Waiting.

Waltters and DeLeu. *God Is Like . . .* (Ave Maria Press). Age 2 and up. Rock, wind, light, water.

Water

Cole. *When the Tide Is Low* (L. L. & S.). Age 3 and up. Water soothes and cools.

dePaola.* *Noah and the Ark* (Winston Press). Age 3 and up. Noah's story.

Hines. *Taste the Raindrops* (Greenwillow). Age 3 and up. Mother–child play.

Raffi. *Bathtime* (Four Winds). Age 1 and up. Cleans.

Shulevitz. *Rain Rain Rivers* (FSG). Age 2 and up. Rain; water.

Van Leeuwen. *Too Hot for Ice Cream* (Dial). Age 3 and up. Cools; heals.

Vashima. *Umbrella* (Puffin). Age 3 and up. Wonderment.

Light

Dragonwagon. *When Light Turns into Night* (Harper and Row). Age 4 and up. Aloneness; belonging.

Grifalconi. *Darkness and the Butterfly* (L. B. & Company). Age 4 and up. Light; fear of dark.

Heide. *It Never Is Dark* (Follett). Age 3 and up. Light at night.

Hoban. *Amy Loves the Sun* (Harper and Row). Age 1 and up. Enjoying the sun.

McMillan. *Growing Colors* (L. L. & S.). Age 1 and up. Colors.

Ray. *Star-Gazing Sky* (Crown). Age 2 and up. Wonder of the stars.

Rylant. *Night in the Country* (Bradbury). Age 2 and up. Dark; light; sounds.

Shulevitz. *Dawn* (Farrar, Straus & Giroux). Age 2 and up. Experiencing dawn with Grandfather.

Fire

LeGuin. *Fire and Stone* (Atheneum). Age 4 and up. Love and understanding conquer fear.

Lewis. *Hill of Fire* (Harper Trophy). Age 3 and up. Destruction; rebuilding.

Scheck.* *The Water That Caught on Fire* (Arch/Concordia). Age 3 and up. God is real.

Wind

Dragonwagon. *Wind Rose* (Harper and Row). Age 4 and up. Child's conception of wind.

Mazumura. *I See the Winds* (Crowell). Age 3 and up. What the wind moves.

McKissack and Pinkney. *Mirandy and Brother Wind* (Knopf). Age 5 and up. Rural African American South.

Food

Aliki. *Corn Is Maize: The Gift of the Indians* (Harper and Row). Age 3 and up. Corn.

dePaola. *Watch Out for the Chicken Feet in Your Soup* (Greenwillow). Age 3 and up. Italian Nonna feeds a child's friends.

Greeley. *Where's My Share?* (Macmillan). Age infant and up. Animals' food.

LeBar.* *How God Gives Us Bread* (Standard Publishing). Age 3 and up. Bread.

Lindsey. *When Batistine Made Bread* (Macmillan). Age 4 and up. From seed to loaf.

Sawyer. *Journey Cakes Ho!* (Viking). Age 3 and up. Food for the journey.

Table Fellowship

Friedman. *How My Parents Learned to Eat* (Houghton Mifflin). Age 3 and up. Japanese-American life.

Galdone. *The Little Red Hen* (Clarion). Age 2 and up. Mutual service; table sharing.

Isadora. *The Potter's Kitchen* (Greenwillow). Age 3 and up. Family kitchen.

Polushkin. *Bubba and Babba* (Crown). Age 3 and up. Laziness; repentance; sharing a meal.

Raffi. *Mealtime* (Four Winds). Age 1 and up. Baby eats.

Sadler. *The Rabbit and the Turnip* (Doubleday). Age 3 and up. Sharing.

Webber. *The Winter Picnic* (Pantheon). Age 2 and up. Mother–child winter picnic.

Caring and Compassion

deKort.* *The Good Samaritan* (Augsburg). Age 2 and up. Neighbor. Also *The Blind Man* (Augsburg). Age 2 and up. Miracle. Also *Jesus and a Little Girl* (Augsburg). Age 2 and up. Miracle.

Galdone. *Little Tuppen* (Clarion). Age 3 and up. Community's gift for the sick.

Hansen-Cole.* *Pablo and the Miracle of St. Anton* (St. Anthony Messenger Press). Age 4 and up. Miracle.

Palau. *Our Teddies, Our Selves* (Little, Brown). Age 4 and up. Taking care of Teddy.

Rockwell. *The Emergency Room* (Macmillan). Age 4 and up. Experiencing the emergency room. Also *Sick in Bed* (Macmillan). Age 3 and up. Child deals with strep throat.

Wiseman. *Morris the Mouse Has a Cold* (Macmillan). Age 3 and up. Humor; care taking.

Seeds and Other Growing Things

Carle, E. *The Tiny Seed* (Scholastic). Age 1 and up. Beautiful art; egg to butterfly; delightful.

Dunn. *The Little Duck, the Little Lamb* (Random House). Age 3 and up. Follows the duck and the lamb from prenatal to grown-ups.

Ernst. *Nattie Parson's Good Luck Lamb* (Viking). Age 5 and up. Lamb/child growth.

Hutchins. *Titch* (Macmillan). Age 1 and up. Little is important.

Kraus. *The Carrot Seed* (Harper and Row). Age 2 and up. Faith; seed.

Parry.* *The Farmer and the Seed* (Augsburg). Age 1 and up. Parable of the Good Ground.

Rylant. *This Year's Garden* (Bradbury Press). Age 3 and up. Family garden.

Teachers

Caudill. *Pocketful of Cricket* (H. R. W.). Age 5 and up. Understanding; caring.

Cohen. *Even Higher* (L. L. & S.). Age 4 and up. Robin's authenticity (God and the poor).

dePaola. *The Art Lesson* (Holiday House). Age 5 and up. Teacher rigidity.

Johnson. *Mother Seton Starts a School* (Winston). Age 4 and up. Story of Mother Seton.

Yashima. *Crow Boy* (Viking). Age 5 and up. Teacher "sees" hidden child.

Scripture

Henley Davis.* *The Beginner's Bible* (Questar). Age 2 and up. Excellent, timeless children's stories.

L'Engle and Giotto. *The Glorius Impossible* (Simon and Schuster). Age 3 and up. Story and art.

Work

Barton. *Building a House* (Greenwillow). Age 2 and up. House building.

Brodsky. *Jonah, an Old Testament Story* (Lippincott). Age 4 and up. Story of the prophet.

Burton. *Katy and the Big Snow* (Houghton Mifflin). Age 3 and up. Snow plow. Also *Mike Mulligan and the Steam Shovel* (Houghton Mifflin). Age 3 and up. Steam Shovel.

Carle. *A Very Busy Spider* (Philomel). Age infant an up. Concentration.

Cooney. *Miss Rumphius* (Viking/Puffin). Age 4 and up. Making beauty.

Ets. *Mister Penny* (Viking). Age 4 and up. Lazy to cooperative.

Holzenthaler. *My Hands Can* (Dutton). Age 2 and up. Learning to "do" various things.

Klug. *I'm a Good Helper* (Augsburg). Age 3 and up. Helping/Christian.

Krasilovsky. *The Man Who Didn't Wash His Dishes* (Doubleday). Age 3 and up. Doing dishes.

Lionni. *Frederick* (Pantheon). Age 3 and up. Storyteller. Also *Matthew's Dream* (Pantheon). Age 3 and up. Artist.

Morgan. *The Turnip* (Philomel). Age 2 and up. Little help is big!

Piper. *The Little Engine* (Scholastic). Age 2 and up. Perseverance.

Scarry, R. *What Do People Do All Day?* (Random House). Age 2 and up. Many jobs.

Slobodkina. *Caps for Sale* (Scholastic). Age 2 and up. Communication.